MONMOUTH SCHOOL
AND
MONMOUTH

1614 - 1995

William Jones, Merchant Adventurer and Freeman of the
Worshipful Company of Haberdashers

MONMOUTH SCHOOL
AND
MONMOUTH

1614 - 1995

by

Keith Kissack

LAPRIDGE PUBLICATIONS
1995

First published in 1995 by
Lapridge Publications
25 Church Street
Hereford HR1 2LR

ISBN 0 9518589 8 X

Printed in Great Britain by
Biddles Ltd. of Guildford

CONTENTS

AUTHOR'S PREFACE

'A good school story will never be written, because nothing ever happens at school'.
(C.H. Cullingford, Speech Day, 1948)

This is largely because so much has to be kept quiet. But the problem arising from the establishment of a grammar school to teach the classics to free boys from a small, unenlightened community, and the ensuing conflicts between parents, teachers, a distant London company and a variety of educational authorities, is of interest because Monmouth was not unique. Many similar towns were faced with the same problem: how to reconcile the classical curriculum with the purpose of the charity.

Of course things happened, and it has been the contention between Catholics and Puritans, between the Worshipful Company of Haberdashers and the school, between the school and the town, between masters and parents, and between headmasters and mayors that makes the story interesting. That is what this book is about.

Keith Kissack, Monmouth, 1995

ACKNOWLEDGEMENTS

I am grateful to many people: to Rupert Lane, the late headmaster, who commissioned the book; to Sheila van Moyland, Richard Beech, Pamela Woods, Robert Glover, Clifford Tucker, Adrian Barlow, Jonathan Holmes, and David Jenkins; to the librarians and archivists, Andrew Dixon, Caroline Hargaden and Merrilyn Tucker; to the Haberdashers' archivist John Cope; to all previous writers on the school, especially W.M.Warlow, Harold Ward and Ian Archer; to Andrew Helme and the staff of the Monmouth Museum; to Geoffrey Webb for illustrating the theme of this book so concisely; to TRIPE for inside information; to Tim Pridgeon for making the usually stressful business of publication so congenial; and to my wife for once again graciously weathering the disruption which writing such a book as this always entails.

Abbreviations used in the the references which follow each chapter

MB.	*Monmouthshire Beacon*
SLB.	School letter books
SVB.	School visitors' books
VA.	Vizard archives
GL.	Guildhall Library
BL.	British Library
MM.	*Monmouthshire Merlin*
MG.	*Monmouthshire Gazette*
MBA.	Monmouth borough archives
LB.	Lecturers' books
MCA.	Monmouthshire county archives
SA.	School archives

Glossary

(Butler) Education Act (1944) Proposed three types of state school: grammar, technical and modern; raised leaving age to fifteen; abolished fees for secondary education

charity In this case, the Worshipful Company of Haberdashers, which acted as trustee and executor to fulfil the wills of its members

direct grant school An annual payment allowed under the 1944 Education Act for each pupil over 11 in fee-charging schools, in return for local education authority access to 25 per cent of the places

endowed school A school set up by and receiving regular income from a private benefactor or group such as a charity or trade association

free pupil A pupil whose fees were paid by the endowment (see above)

grammar school Originally an ecclesiastical establishment in which candidates for the priesthood learned Latin; in mediaeval times, usually founded (as in Monmouth's case) by private benefactors, church bodies or trade guilds

haberdasher A merchant dealing in dressmaking cloths, accessories and sewing goods; their trade association petitioned the aldermen of London in 1371 for recognition as a guild, was granted a coat of arms in 1446, and as the Guild of St Katherine the Virgin of the Haberdashers of the City of London acquired a meeting hall in 1458

high school A higher secondary school; a grammar school; a grammar school which became a comprehensive school may have incorporated 'high' in its name

independent (school) Not supported by public funds

lecturer Originally senior to the headmaster at Monmouth; described by William Jones the founder as a preacher, latterly known as warden, and by Dr Johnson as 'One who instructs insolently and dogmatically'

liveryman One entitled to wear the livery or uniform of the Haberdashers, granted in 1448

New Scheme Used loosely to describe any decree altering the way in which schools were run and teaching carried out; the National Curriculum is a modern example

public school Usually an ancient grammar school which became 'public' through its ability to attract pupils from beyond its local area

recusant One who from the time of Elizabeth I declined to attend the parish church; often but not exclusively a reference to Roman Catholics

usher A lower master; a 'drudge', according to Dr Johnson

Welsh Intermediate Education Act (1869) Allowed local councils to levy a rate of a halfpenny in the pound to pay for intermediate education

INTRODUCTION

William Jones, a man with connections in both Monmouth and Newland, but who had spent most of his life abroad, was invited in 1600 to become a member of the livery of the Worshipful Company of Haberdashers. He died childless fifteen years later, having left £9000 to that company 'to ordaine a Preacher, a Free-School, and Almes-houses for twenty poor and old distressed people, as blind and lame, as it shall seem best to them, of the Towne of Monmouth, where it shall be bestowed'.[1]

What little is known of the benefactor's life comes from Thomas Fuller who wrote *The History of the Worthies of England* within fifty years of William Jones's death. It is a fanciful account and the source of most of the legends which have followed:

> 'William Jones was a native to Monmouth, a person whose estate was very considerable in some respects, viz: In, First, his Emptiness, being forced out of Monmouth for not being able to pay ten groats, as the late Recorder of that Corporation hath informed me ... Secondly his Filling: flying to London, he became first a porter, and then, (his brains being better than his back), a factor and going over to Hamburgh, by his industry and ingenuity made such a vent for Welsh cottons, that what he found drugs at home he left dainties beyond the sea. Thirdly his Refunding; founding a fair School House in the place of his nativity, allowing £50 yearly for the Master, £30 for the Usher, with 100 marks salary for a Lecturer. Besides a stately Almshouse for twenty poor folk, each of them having two rooms and a garden with half a crown a week, besides other conveniences'.[2]

What is not clear from the little that is known about William Jones is why he bequeathed almost half his fortune of £40 000 to charity. The fact that he seems to have been unmarried helped, as did the hope, expressed in his will, that Christ would raise his 'body and soul into everlasting life at the last day of judgment'. But his generosity was more than a passport to Paradise. There was purpose behind it. His grants to lecturers and his emphasis on schools reveal a man with strong views on the importance of good works. His eagerness to evangelise the Marches of Wales where recusancy survived, where a Member of Parliament claimed that 'the prayers of the common people are more like spells and charms than devotion', was the expression of his strong Puritan belief. Whatever his motives, that share of his charity which he allotted to Monmouth has been of invaluable benefit to many people.

The letters patent, which the company had to obtain from the King, changed 'Free-School' to 'Free Grammar School', and the statutes of 1616 then provided the rules by which the school was to be run. The latter went into considerable detail, emphasising that the school should be free for all children, 'especially such as are born within the said town of Monmouth, and then for others born within the said county'. There was however an admission fee of sixpence for poor children and two shillings for the rest. These were perquisites for the master who took two-thirds and for the usher who took one-third. Such admission fees could be a source of contention in a nominally free school and Monmouth was no exception. The school could have up to 100 children but the master and usher were the only members of the teaching staff. They received respectively thirty and twenty days holiday in the year.

Before they could be appointed, four plots of land on the river bank, consisting of three houses, a barn and meadows had to be bought for £100. Buildings had then to be designed, bricklayers brought from London, local lawyers dealt with, and those inhabitants of Monmouth whose view of the river, the bridge, the weir, and the Kymin was being obstructed, pacified. The man responsible for all this, for enduring endless journeys from London, for settling local quarrels, placating the bricklayers who thought they were being underpaid, and satisfying the preacher's requirements for his house, was the company clerk, Basil Nicholl. His worth was belatedly recognised by the company when they awarded him £100 because 'he bestoweth almost his whole tyme in the affaires and busynesses of this Company, the profittes of his Clarkship (being) scarcely sufficient to defray his household expences'.[3]

Small though these early buildings were, the insertion of such a complex of school, twenty almshouses and three staff dwellings between this fairly primitive little market town and the river on which its trades had relied for so long, must have seemed like the coming of the A40 to later generations. But they were quickly accepted. What friction arose over William Jones's bequest, came from the interpretation of his will by the company; the status of the preacher and his relationship with the headmaster, the usher and the local vicar; and from the meaning of 'free school', what it should teach, and where the children should come from. A further matter, soon settled by the company, was the fact that the cost exceeded the money available by £1680. Of a more permanent nature was the obligation of preacher, master and usher to keep their houses in repair. This was something they rarely did, and it caused many disputes between them, their successors, and the company.

The Old Schoolroom

While the buildings were rising the three appointments were being made. They were to introduce into a strongly Catholic area the opinions of a London company with equally strong Protestant tendencies. Monmouthshire had more convicted recusants (117 per 1000 of the population) than any other county. In Monmouth itself the priory had been occupied by recusants since 1572, almost all the farms in the Monnow valley were owned by recusants, there was a Jesuit headquarters at The Cwm, and the most important local landowners, the Somersets, Herberts, Morgans and Vaughans, were equally anti-Puritan. It had been acknowledged for some time that, 'few causes arose in the Shire which are not made a question between Protestant and Recusant', and as disruptive elements, Puritan preachers were the most likely to cause trouble. Laud called them 'the people's creatures'.

They soon came to be known as lecturers and were introduced, not only to spread Protestant belief, but to oppose popery and superstition. They were independent of bishops and the local clergy, and Charles I described them as 'furious promoters of the most dangerous innovations'. The Monmouth letters patent gives no indication of such dangers, asking only for 'one honest, sufficient and approved learned man', being at least a Master of Arts of Oxford or Cambridge, 'to perform divine service in any church within the same town, or in the almshouses'. He could be dismissed for being absent for forty days in any one year, for adultery, drunkenness and for accepting another benefice. Twice a year he was to visit the school, examine the scholars, and report in writing to the company 'any negligence or insufficiency... that order may be taken for reformation therein'. Not mentioned in the document was how the relationships between the lecturer and the local vicar were to be accommodated. He was given a house and garden and a salary of 100 marks (£66 13s 4d) a year. This was to increase slowly to £100 in 1714, to £140 in 1822, to £175 in 1841, and to £200 with £200 allowances in 1870.

The master was less important, and until 1841 this was reflected in his lower salary of £60, but by 1870 he was getting £264 10s a year with £152 allowances. He had a house and garden, as did the usher whose salary had risen from £30 in 1616 to £130 in 1841. It was the master's duty to teach the usher 'his trade in teaching' and together they were responsible for all instruction and discipline. They were to be inspected once a year by 'men of good conscience and judgment, who shall observe how the children profit, and what the Master and Usher have done in keeping these orders'. So with both the preacher and the men of good conscience issuing reports on the staff and scholars, the company was able to exercise firm, if remote, control.

The usher, at the bottom of the scale, could confide his troubles to his diary, and they were many. Doctor Johnson was for a short time an usher at a private school and described it as painful drudgery, 'as unvaried as the note of the cuckow'. He did not know whether it was more disagreeable for him to teach, or the boys to learn. 'Vitam continet una dies', he wrote, 'one day contains the whole of my life'. The Monmouth ushers probably found it very similar. The sole attraction was the hope that the post might prove a stepping stone to the headmastership.

The children were to arrive at 7 a.m., 'decently and cleanly apparelled' and the day began with 'a Godly prayer'. Work continued until 11 when a portion out of the New Testament in Greek or Latin was read, and dinner was eaten. Work began again at 12.30 and continued until 5 p.m. when a chapter of the Bible was read, prayers said, and a psalm sung. Each boy was to have a Bible or service book for these occasions; all had to be catechised once a week; and everyone attended church on Sundays and holy days. The Bible was to be the Authorised Version of 1611, probably the greatest set-book ever used in a school, containing only six thousand different words (Shakespeare used three times as many). But as Christopher Hill has remarked, it could also provide rhetorical justification for almost any radical view, political, economic, or religious.[4] Lecturers at the school were quick to make use of it.

The school was to be divided into not more than six classes, the boys moving from one to another in accordance with their 'sound knowledge in reading and writing, understanding and penning of the English, Latin and Greek tongues, both in prose and verse'. It was customary for the usher to teach the three lower forms from Lily's Brevissima Institutio, and for the headmaster to take the upper three classes in Latin and Greek. To attain purity in Latin, Tully and Caesar were to be the patterns for prose, and Terence and Virgil for verse. No author who might 'hinder goodness or religion' was to be allowed. There were to be half-holidays from 2 p.m. on Thursday and annual holidays at Christmas, Easter and Whitsun. The length of these holidays continued to nettle the locals throughout the centuries.

Master and usher were to keep weekly corrections and chastise anyone guilty of those 'vices which reign amongst the ignorant and profane multitude, as swearing, filthy talking, cursed speaking, contention, gaming, unthriftiness and the like; the which being disclosed, they shall in no case suffer to escape punishment'. If flogging failed, expulsion followed. This was to be a continuing source of conflict between masters and parents and eventually between school and town.

A precedent had been created at the neighbouring free school in Newland, a village where William Jones endowed another preacher and almshouses. That school had been founded in the late fifteenth century and in the decade in which Monmouth was founded the Newland headmaster, Thomas Jauncey, took a parent to the Court of Star Chamber for assaulting him because he had administered to his sons 'such correction as they deserved'.[5] There is no record of the outcome of this case, but flogging was to arouse passionate advocates and opponents well into the twentieth century. Doctor Johnson put the problem concisely in 1775 when he claimed that, due to a decline in beating, children learned less, 'so that what boys gain at one end they lose at the other'.

One might well ask what were the alternatives to the robust regime of a local grammar school. The wealthy could send their sons to Eton, Winchester or a tutor, though the result might not always be advantageous. Bishop Burnet, in the late seventeenth century, thought the English gentry 'for the most part the worst instructed and the least knowing of any of their rank, I ever went amongst'.[6] For the sons of the middling sort there were only two, the petty school which taught reading and writing to those under eight, and the writing master who would teach English from a daily chapter of the Bible, writing, a little arithmetic, and, according to Richard Hoole, a future Monmouth headmaster, 'such preparative arts as may make them (the children) completely fit to undergoe any calling'.

When the school was founded Monmouth had been the county town for over three-quarters of a century. As such it was fulfilling two of the requirements of such places; it was the headquarters of the militia, and the seat of the assizes. Through the generosity of William Jones it acquired a third ingredient, the grammar school. This then combined the objectives of those two earlier elements in the motto which it took from the arms of the Haberdashers' Company, 'Serve and Obey'. And so long as Monmouth remained the county town, the school was to retain a link with the assizes through 'The Judge's Half', a holiday granted by the visiting judges in acknowledgement of a request in Latin by the head of the school.

References

[1] £6000 had already been handed to the company in 1613: the remaining £3000 was granted in the will.

[2] Published in 1662 after his death.

[3] I.W. Archer, *The History of the Haberdashers' Company*, (Phillimore, 1991), 55.

[4] C. Hill, *The English Bible and the Seventeenth Century Revolution*, (Allen Lane, 1993).

[5] *Catalogue of Star Chamber Proceedings relating to Wales*, (Cardiff, 1929), 191.

[6] *History of My Own Times*, 1724.

1 THE FIRST FIFTY YEARS: 1615-1666

In the Spring of 1615 the first three appointments were made; John Owen as master, Richard Owen as usher, and Robert Sedgwick as lecturer. Two of them were to prove a disappointment, only the usher surviving for more than two years. But it was not an easy time to found a school, the Lord Privy Seal in 1610 stating that there was 'nothing so hurtful to the Commonwealth as the multitude of free schools', sending boys out to an easy life at a university from which they returned 'to breed new opinions'.

The chief 'breeder of new opinions' in Monmouth was to be the lecturer. He had been a friend of William Jones, was an overseer of his will under which he received a legacy of £150, and was probably chosen for the post by the founder himself. However he arrived in Monmouth to find a certain John Hughes already acting as lecturer. There seems some doubt as to who had appointed him, but the matter was quickly settled by the company, Mr. Hughes reluctantly accepting a redundancy payment of £5 and moving away.

Sedgwick was to last only two years but they were enough for him to create considerable disturbance in a fairly reactionary neighbourhood. He had been trained at Peterhouse where the influence of the master was strongly Puritan. He acquired a living in Kent but lost it for criticising the prebends of Canterbury. He became a private chaplain but was dismissed because of his preaching in Battersea. A friend managed to get him abroad, and eventually to Hamburg where he became preacher and met Jones. Here he introduced 'a purer discipline ... and the Lord abundantly blessed his labours'. His stay in Monmouth ended in 1617 when he became preacher at Wapping Chapel. There he was cited for not using the Book of Common Prayer, for not administering communion and for having no communion rails.[1]

Lectureships were essentially Puritan institutions in which city companies provided the money which parishes could not afford. In Monmouth Sedgwick seems to have kept to the school. Other Puritans went further afield, and Walter Powell of Llantilio, who sent his five sons 'John, Wm, Tho, Rich and Charles to Monmouth free Scoole' in August 1628, frequently complained to his diary of Puritans like John Morgan, preaching 'damnacion to Llantilio people'.[2]

John Owen, M.A., the first headmaster, was equally transitory. He was in holy orders and obtained powerful references from both the Lord Chancellor and the Lord Chief Justice. But, considering that his appointment was to set up a well-endowed new school, he acted with such lack of enthusiasm and energy that after two years he was summoned to London to answer the charge that, through his negligence, 'the School is much disgraced, the number of scholars there decreased, and the Town of Monmouth greatly hindered'. It is not clear what the hindrance was, but the company had written to the mayor asking him his opinion of Owen's 'demeanour and carriage in the place of a schoolmaster', and his answer may have caused the trouble. Owen abjectly confessed that he was 'unable to take the paynes which that place required', and resigned.

As a result, Humfrey Crewys, a fellow of King's College, Cambridge was appointed, only to find that John Owen had changed his mind and written a letter revoking his resignation and enclosing letters from 'dyvers of the towne of Monmouth on his behalfe'. The problem was passed by the company to their invaluable clerk, so Basil Nicholl accompanied Mr. Crewys to Monmouth to ensure that he could get into his house. Mr. Owen was waiting for them with a scheme to persuade Mr. Crewys to surrender one-third of his salary of £60 for the next three years. When this was reluctantly agreed, Owen was encouraged to ask for it in a lump sum so that he could purchase a benefice. Although this was refused, the request created a precedent which was to cause much trouble in the future, masters amassing benefices to supplement their salary. Although the company disapproved, Monmouth maintained that it would get a better type of master if it was allowed.

Lecturers, too, tended to disregard the rules. Robert Brabourne succeeded Sedgwick on 5 August 1617. The company seems to have reacted against Sedgwick's radicalism by appointing a man whose royalist feelings were to emerge in the Civil War. As a precaution he was put on two years probation, the company agreeing that 'if his good life and profitable preaching' was then approved, he could have the post for life. Approval was given in 1619 and in that year he became vicar of Monmouth, with the chapel of St. Thomas ultra pontem. He was the first of several to combine the two posts, admitting that although the vicar's salary was only £22, the addition of the lecturer's £66 13s 4d provided the makings of a reasonable living. Brabourne was an astute tactician and was one of the few who managed to act at various times as lecturer, vicar, usher and headmaster.

Meanwhile, Mr. Crewys was beginning to feel his age and this had become known to a Mr. Jones who, claiming to keep a grammar school near Hereford, offered himself as an assistant in the hope that he might step into Crewys's shoes when he died. The company would have nothing to do with this, but in 1636 Mr. Crewys offered to give up half his salary to acquire an assistant and Nathaniel Taynton was appointed. This infuriated the usher, William Voyle, who had succeeded Richard Owen in 1623. He seems to have hoped for the appointment in spite of a singularly uneventful spell of duty in which he had been absent on many occasions, far in excess of his permitted twenty days. Without telling the company, he departed for Cheshire and is not heard of again. He was followed by Peter Gough, an usher who owing to 'the troubles in these parts' was also often absent.

In 1639 Mr. Crewys died and Nathaniel Taynton was appointed headmaster. Three years later Charles I raised the royal standard at Nottingham and Parliament responded locally by ordering the mayor to remove the militia stores from Monmouth Castle to Newport. The mayor refused, as did several councillors and three magistrates. As a result the mayor and councillors were imprisoned in London and the magistrates were dismissed. For the next few years the school, the company and the town entered on a period of conflicting political and religious turbulence.

School and town were to survive through a judicious mixture of maximum discretion and minimum valour. As a result, Monmouth's seeming neutrality became notorious to both sides. 'I was never in so base a place in all my life', wrote a Royalist officer in 1644, and some years later Major-General Berry, a notable Parliamentary general, described the inhabitants as 'Pitiful people ... who served with both hands ... Vices abounding ... magistrates fast asleep'. Apathy was to be followed by armed neutrality when groups of farmers and tradesmen, tired of watching their fields and property looted by both sides, banded together as 'country clubmen' to keep both King and Parliament as far from Monmouth as possible. They had limited success and the town changed hands several times. As a result, the school, relative newcomers, run by a London company with its own Parliamentary militia, receiving boys from a strongly Royalist and recusant area, had to exercise extreme discretion both politically and socially.

This was made more difficult by the fact that the most powerful local commander, Colonel Kyrle of Walford Court, had a brother at the school. The colonel changed sides at least twice and proved a particular cause of trouble to the usher, More Pye, who had succeeded Peter Gough in 1646. In the following year he went to Walford to collect the brother's school fees and was repulsed. He then sent his servant Joan 'with 200 oysters 6d. Her passage over Wye 2d.' and eventually received the £5 for the boy's half-year diet. More Pye kept not only a diary but also a private boarding house on the Causey (Monnow Street).

He was a hypochondriac, constantly bewailing his ill-health. On one occasion he went to the doctor, complaining of 'choaking cold and abundance of watery flegm' and, when told he was in a dangerous consumption, inscribed unsteadily, 'Lord God prepare me for Heaven'. He was equally concerned about the health of his boys for whom he bought quantities of worm-seeds and treacle.

When not dosing the boys he was trying to keep them under control. Having given Charles Herbert, a boy from a local Parliamentary family, six verses, the boy ran off without leave to the leaguer where the usher found him drinking 'with a bowe of birch in his hands ... all wet and daubed with dirt'. He got away to Monnow Street and in a long report to the headmaster, More Pye described how he found him bullying a boy, pulling off his bands, throwing dirt in his mouth and beating him, so that 'He never came within doores till eight att night, after we had all supt and ready to go to bed. Next morning hee went out before I was up, in all ye raine, and came not in till Saturday night, about 7 o'clock'.

He rarely refers to the Civil War unless he is complaining about the cost of quartering the soldiers. He kept his feelings to himself until the King escaped from Hampton Court when he wrote exultantly, 'Vivat, vivat, vivat in aeternum'. He briefly described the last days: 'March 30 (1647) Colonel Kyrle came to Monmouth and gave orders for the slighting of the garrison ... about £100 imposed as a loan upon the town for payment of the soldiers' arrears ... the townsmen and soldiers began to pull down the round tower of the Castle and to demolish the works'. On the Sunday before Christmas, 'about twelve o'clock, the Tower of the castle of Monmouth fell down upon one side, whilst we were at sermon'.[3]

In the early days of the Commonwealth Mr. Brabourne was ejected from the vicarage of Monmouth by the Committee for Plundered Ministers on the grounds of malignancy and scandal. In consequence he also had to forfeit the lectureship. In the same year (1652) More Pye resigned and, after an interval, was followed as usher by the first old boy to receive a Leaving Exhibition to Oxford, John Crumpe. The replacement of the lecturer was more difficult. Cromwell, by letter, had recommended Roger Charnock, but the company was reluctant to appoint him until they had heard him preach a trial sermon. This proved acceptable and he was put on probation for two years.

As no vicar replaced Mr. Brabourne until 1657, it seems to have been assumed that Mr. Charnock would carry out the necessary duties at the parish church, but at the end of the two years the company was disturbed to hear that he had not administered either communion or baptism and that one of his own children was not baptised. Charnock duly confessed, made some unsatisfactory excuses, and was granted one more year to prove his worth. At the end of the period, he was summoned to London where he arrived, armed with a second testimonial from Cromwell. It was difficult for the company to ignore the Lord Protector, but the appointment was only confirmed when Mr. Charnock promised to administer the sacraments.

In 1657 Nathaniel Taynton died. He seems to have weathered the Civil War and the interregnum with tact and skill, neither town nor company complaining of his conduct. This was in spite of being assisted by Robert Brabourne who, on removal from the lectureship, had bided his time until 1655 when he managed to get himself appointed usher. He was thus in position to step into the headmaster's shoes when he died, and this he quickly did. He then unwisely accepted a parish in Herefordshire, and the company was immediately told of this by the recorder of Monmouth, who for some time acted as an informer to the company. He went on to amplify local concern over the way the school 'was suffered every day to decay and be worse and worse' owing to Mr. Brabourne's inefficiency. The headmaster was by then at least seventy and, on dismissal, glad to retire from the hurly-burly of the classroom to the deep peace of a Herefordshire vicarage.

As Mr. Charnock also had died there were now two vacancies. The vicar of Newland, who acted as another company double-agent, proposed Nicholas Carey, a Gloucestershire minister, for the post of lecturer as 'he would be a notable instrument of good to the town of Monmouth'. He was approved, as was Robert Frampton who was recommended as headmaster by the recorder, burgesses and gentry of Monmouth. Neither was to last long.

Frampton got off to a good start, increasing the number of boys considerably, but for Carey progress was blocked by Mr. Charnock's widow, still firmly entrenched in the lecturer's house. She had done nothing to keep it in repair, had paid no rent, and firmly refused to leave. She remained immovable for nine months until, in desperation, the company offered her £5 and she departed.

When Cromwell died in 1658 the company was heavily in debt. Vast loans to the Government during the Civil War remained unpaid, over £700-worth of the Haberdashers' plate had been sold, while ship money, the rising cost of the militia and increasing taxation meant that many members put their hopes of financial salvation in the restoration of the monarchy.

In Monmouth, similar feelings were afoot. Ten years before the school was founded, James I had given the town a new charter of incorporation in order that the borough should, 'at all perpetual future times ... be and remain a town of Peace

The Haberdashers' earliest grant of arms in 1446 featured three Katherine wheels for the company's patron saint who was tortured in this way. In 1502, on being incorporated as Merchant Haberdashers, they partly exchanged the cult of their saint for commerce, and adopted a new coat of arms with a leopard to show royal patronage and a field of blue and silver for their overseas trade. The supporters, two Indian goats, and a crest with arms holding a garland were added later. The arms and motto, 'Serve and Obey', were eventually adopted by all the Haberdasher schools.

William Jones's coat of arms, the origin of the present school crest

and Quiet, to the example and terror of the wicked and the reward of the Good'.[4] At the school, peace and quiet had rarely been notable, and according to the usher, wickedness had been rife.

Quite apart from the problems of the Civil War, the years between 1640 and 1660 had not been easy ones for any school based on the classics. Many books published at this time were not by academics, but by radicals adapting a close knowledge of the Bible to their political ends.[5] As Bunyan boasted when mocked for his lack of a university education, it was Pilate who could write in Hebrew, Latin and Greek, not Christ's chosen disciples. Even so, as the school neared the end of its first half century, its founder was at last commemorated by a brass plate recording his charitable works, placed over the gate to the foreyard of the school, and by a framed portrait hanging in the school hall.

The present painting is a copy of the original in the Haberdashers' Hall. In 1841 it was in 'a neglected state' and sent to London for restoration.[6] It was still there in 1847,[7] but eventually came back to the school.

References

[1] P. Seaver, *The Puritan Lectureships*, (Stamford, 1970).
[2] *The Diary of Walter Powell, 1603-1654*, (ed. Bradney, 1907).
[3] Extracts from the lost diary in MB. 9/7/1859.
[4] MBA. 2/12/1605.
[5] C. Hill, *op. cit.*
[6] SVB. 3/3/1841.
[7] SVB. 22/6/1847.

2 THE SCHOOL UNDER THE LATER STUARTS: 1666-1714

When Charles II arrived in London to reclaim the throne in 1660, John Evelyn was watching in the Strand. 'Bless God', he wrote, 'and all this was done without one drop of blood shed, and by that very army which rebelled against him'. At the school too, hopes of reconciliation were high. Mr. Frampton had abandoned his benefices, raised the numbers so he claimed to over a hundred, introduced a register of scholars, and was acclaimed by the company for 'his care and diligence in advancing the repute of the School'.

Although Charles confirmed the charter of James I, peace and quiet were not to be the characteristics of the next half century either. In spite of Mr. Frampton's early success, complaints from Monmouth about the decline of the school and the reduction in the numbers 'by reason of the neglect of the present Schoolmaster' had reached London by 1662. Mr. Frampton quickly persuaded his local friends to repudiate this and the company received a letter from the mayor and bailiffs giving an account of 'the learned exercises' shown by the scholars at the mayoral election.[1] The writers went on to commend the master's honesty and ability and denied that any of the complaints to the company had come from them. London then adopted the curious policy of asking Robert Brabourne, the retired headmaster, to adjudicate, so Mr. Frampton, who knew him and scented danger, sent in his resignation, 'by reason of several ecclesiastical preferments'.

Before he left there was trouble with the lecturer, Nicholas Carey. In 1662 the Act of Uniformity ordered all clergymen of the Church of England to conform to the laws and regulations of the Book of Common Prayer. The mayor and burgesses promptly wrote to the company stating that, as Mr. Carey refused to conform to the Act, he could no longer be the lecturer. At the same time they recommended his replacement by Charles Godwin, 'a man of pious life, great learning and orthodox carriage'. The company agreed and the vicar of Newland, who had proposed Carey, took pity on him and employed him with the almspeople there.

In 1663 John Harmer, who had been Professor of Greek at Oxford, was appointed headmaster. But not for long. He seems to have arrived in Monmouth, looked around, had second thoughts, and resigned, the company reluctantly paying him £5, the cost of the journey. They also gave £5 to the usher, Saul Jordan, who had succeeded Brabourne in 1657 and through all these comings and goings had been teaching the school single-handed. He continued to do so until a replacement was

25

found. This was to be Charles Hoole, a London schoolmaster with, according to the mayor, 'great abilities and qualifications'. His qualifications were mainly as an educationalist and as the writer of numerous books on how to teach. As a result he had little time to practise that art and assumed that the usher, who already had considerable experience in teaching the whole school on his own, could continue to do so.

Amongst the seventeen books by Mr. Hoole, mentioned in the Dictionary of National Biography, are *A New Discovery of the Old Art of Teaching Schoole* in 1640, *An Easy Entrance to the Latin Tongue* in 1649, Lily's *Latin Grammar fitted for the use in Schooles* in 1653, an edition of the New Testament in Greek in 1664, *Terminationes et Exempla Decliniatorum et Conjugationem in usum Grammaticastorum* in 1650 (it continued to be reprinted many times up to 1857), *Aesop's Fables* in English and Latin in 1700, and *Pueriles Confabulatiunculae, Children's Talk, so that children by the help of their Mother-Tongue may more easily learn to discourse in good Latine among themselves* in 1659.

In the last-named, Mr. Hoole's Battus, who does most of the talking, is an unpleasant child, lazy, dirty, and usually whining about other boys: 'Peter cuft me' (Petrus me cecidit pugnis), 'He pulled my hair', 'He hath bemarred my book', 'John spake English' (lingua vernacula). Reaching school he is met by the master, Fredericus, with 'Come you hither with your staring head of hair'. He disliked games, would not play handball, 'My strength will not abide it', fishing made him wet; he refused to wrestle in case he fell and broke a limb; and he hated riding, swimming ('a dangerous skill') and singing, ('Ego ... abhorrui a canendo'). He was not backward with girls, greeting one of them, 'God save you, pretty lass' (Salve Puella venustissima), to which she replied, 'And you, pretty lad'. Mercifully he was not a Monmothian as the author wrote the book before he came here.[2] The company eventually became aware of this literary activity and Mr. Hoole was dismissed in 1664 for being away from the school from Easter to July, presumably putting the finishing touches to his Greek New Testament.

Both Hoole and Frampton had been appointed by the company on the town's recommendation, and in spite of growing doubts over the wisdom of this system, they appointed William Morrice headmaster on the strength of letters from the Mayor. So they were not pleased to receive in 1671 a flood of complaints from the town about Mr. Morrice's shortcomings. They replied that they would make their own appointments in future and summoned the headmaster to London. He went armed with a sheaf of favourable references and was told to return to Monmouth while the complaints were being examined. While this was being done, more letters arrived from the county magistrates stressing 'his ignorance and insufficiency'. The company then asked the Bishop of Hereford, in whose diocese Monmouth lay, to adjudicate. Foreseeing an unfavourable verdict, Mr. Morrice moved smartly into the neighbouring diocese of Llandaff, where the Bishop of Hereford was powerless, and where he became rector of Mitchel Troy.

On his departure the company, ignoring the town, appointed Thomas Bassett as head. Henry Rogers, the usher, who had hoped for the post, then persuaded Mr. Morrice and 'several persons of Quality' to complain to the company that they had not been consulted and that Mr. Rogers should be appointed. The clerk replied that Mr. Bassett was a master of arts of four years' standing, 'highly recommended for his eminent learning' and so they had thought it just to elect him in their own right.

Trouble then moved to the almshouses over the election of the inmates. Appointments from London, without local consultation, had infuriated the townspeople, but a visit from one of the wardens appeased them by agreeing to retain the old system of the company choosing one of the three names submitted by the council. No such system applied to the election of the lecturer when Charles Godwin died in 1676. Both headmaster and usher applied, but as neither could get to London in time to give a trial sermon, the company appointed John Wickens. The whole town, backed by the Marquess of Worcester, opposed this decision. The vicar, Herbert Pye, who had also hoped for the position, refused to allow the newcomer the use of the pulpit, and dissuaded the Bishop of Hereford from licensing him. So for a time he had to preach in a neighbouring diocese; but opposition must have died down as he remained in office until he resigned in 1685.

Edmund Evans had been appointed usher in 1677, and as there was growing criticism of the state of the school, he was unwisely asked to report privately on its condition and on the abilities of the headmaster. The company could then consider 'the best ways and means for the Recovery of the Schoole to its former Reputation and splendour'. He did this with such relish that the company asked the lecturers of Monmouth and Newland to adjudicate on his report. Bassett's defence prevailed, and the company injudiciously dismissed the usher they had appointed as informer two years earlier.

But Mr. Bassett was faced, on his return, by renewed criticism of the school, and as he had been warned by the company to amend 'his carriage and Demeanour', he was told to return to London and answer the charges. They were sevenfold. He was accused of demanding quarterage from scholars who should be taught free; of acting with severity when administering correction; of having 'a morose and ill humor and carriage'; of 'indulged sloth and negligence'; of his aptness to contend with his usher; of not keeping a house fit to entertain boarders; and of refusing to sit with his scholars in church. He agreed with all charges and asked the court for pardon. He was then addressed by the Master of the Haberdashers ... 'with great prudence and tenderness ... for his future amendment and reformacon'. Bassett grovelled again, thanked the master, and promising to reform in all things, agreed to 'use his utmost endeavors for regaining the credit of the said Schoole by his future diligence and good carriage, both att home and abroad'. The court forgave him and ordered his speedy return to school, unaware of the trouble awaiting him in the backwoods.[3]

He returned to find that most of Monmouth thought it a gross miscarriage of justice. He also found that his old adversary, Evans, was refusing to leave his house, while his replacement as usher, Francis Tyler, was teaching the whole school and living in lodgings. But the old usher had the backing of the mayor and most of the burgesses, who maintained that it was Mr. Evans who had 'by his industry, good behaviour, learning and method of teaching ... raised the Schoole from its late low and despised condition to a good degree of reputacion'. It was a typical example of the difficulties of control when company and school were so far apart. In desperation, the company decided on bribery, and Mr. Evans retired with three years' salary, partly earned barricaded in his house, while Mr. Tyler did the work.

In spite of his unpopularity, Mr. Bassett remained headmaster with the support of the company, but knowledge of his misdeeds did not endear him to his pupils, nor to their parents. As a sop to his critics he did some repairs to his house and presented the school with a bell. He later sent the bill to the company. It was reluctantly paid on condition he did not take the bell with him when he left.

Charles II died in 1685 and was succeeded by James II, regarded by Mr. Bassett as a friend to Rome. Rashly he proceeded to denounce the King to the assembled school. The company quickly summoned him to London when they heard that the King in Council had been informed of 'the Sedicious and Scandalous theame given by Mr. Bassett ... to his Schollars, which reflected upon his present Ma[tie]. when he was Duke of York'.[4]

The headmaster set out for London armed with a copy of what he considered innocent comment, but the company found that his words had been spoken with vicious intentions, and went on to complain about his neglect of duty as a schoolmaster in teaching 'matters that were not fitt to be taught children, but such as were of dangerous consequence to the Government by instilling ill and malicious principles into their minds'.

He was dismissed and returned to Monmouth to enlist the help of the Duke of

Beaufort who put his case to the company. It had little effect and a successor, Thomas Wright, renowned for 'his learning and abilities for teaching school, and also for his sober life and conversation', was appointed. He was told to take up his duties as quickly as possible.

But Mr. Bassett, who had learnt a trick or two from his usher, refused to leave his house on the grounds that, if his words were treasonable, the only person who could eject him was the King. He agreed to leave as soon as a royal command was handed to him. The company appointed a committee to interview the Lord Chancellor who advised them to petition the King. This they did, obtained the order, handed it to Mr. Bassett and he withdrew. He then entered a caveat at the Consistory Court in Hereford, objecting to the licensing of Mr. Wright by the bishop. He was summoned to appear and explain why, but was saved by the Revolution of 1688.

Unfortunately for the company, when James II was driven from the throne, Mr. Bassett quickly acquired a letter from the new King, William of Orange. Armed with this and accompanied by two members of parliament, he returned to London and asked the company to reinstate him. The company was beginning to realise that Mr. Bassett was not to be trifled with, and asked Mr. Wright to attend a court in London. After much debate, Thomas Wright was confirmed in office and told to return to Monmouth.

This he did, but Mr. Bassett was home first, and had procured the help of the usher who 'knocked off the bolts and locks belonging to the sd Schoole and thereby exposed the sd Schoole to the violence of the sd Mr. Bassett's intrusion'. The usher was dismissed and the company took both headmasters to court, where, surprisingly, Mr. Bassett got the verdict. Mr. Wright was appointed head of Bunne Hill School and Mr. Bassett continued to reign in Monmouth until he died in 1713.

But Mr. Tyler was still about and in 1691 wrote apologising for the damage to the locks and bolts and asking for his salary to be paid. The company reluctantly agreed and were happy to see him disappear to the rectory of Wonastow. His place as usher was taken by William Matthews who for twelve years had taught a free school in Worcestershire.

Staff changes were not the only problems affecting Monmouth at the end of the seventeenth century. It was claimed that the almspeople 'did frequently entertain Inmates and such as were of evil fame and loose and disorderly people'. The vicar, Herbert Pye, blamed the lecturer for this failure to control his charges. In 1706 there was trouble in the parish church over light which had been cut off from the school pews by a new gallery. The argument rambled on until 1724 when the church wardens applied to the Bishop of Hereford to prevent the school appropriating the whole gallery.[5] The school responded over a hundred years later, complaining that there were only twenty-eight seats for 100 boys.[6] The outcome of this prolonged dispute was a request from the visitors that the company would provide a chapel 'and make the establishment complete'.[7]

Affairs were little better in a company faced with financial difficulties which could be traced back to the Civil War. The huge loans to the Government had never been repaid, while the destruction of the hall in the Great Fire of 1666 was an added burden. Various remedies were suggested, including the reduction of the salaries of the lecturer and headmaster to £50, but the problem remained.

This was reflected in the state of the school. With so many staff changes, and so much time spent travelling to London to answer complaints, it is difficult to know how much teaching was actually being done. Certainly the old question, of how to accommodate the teaching of the classics to the running of a free charity, remained. But in 1690 John Locke published his Thoughts on Education in which he advocated only so much Latin as the child might need, and that it should be supplemented by drawing, history, arithmetic, astronomy, accounting, gardening and shorthand. He thought Greek, music and fencing unnecessary.

His ideas had no immediate effect in Monmouth, and boys were still copying the school rules in Latin, which included 'Patrium Sermones fugito: Latinum exerce', a hundred years later. Doctor Johnson's short-lived academy, in which Garrick had been a pupil, was still based on Latin and little else, though even he was beginning to see the light, admitting that the most important task of a schoolmaster was 'to attain a habit of expression, without which knowledge is of little use. This is necessary in Latin and more necessary in English'.

But Monmouth, like all grammar schools, was still constricted by its original statutes, and this was especially so when there was trouble with the town, 'for there were persons behind the Curtain that watch all opertunityes to see the Company make a breach in theire own constitutions'.[8] It was not until 1805 that Lord Eldon, adjudicating over the use of Latin at Leeds Grammar School, ruled that statutes which did not permit commercially useful instruction could be changed.

References

[1] It was customary for the senior boys to attend mayor-making ceremonies and for the head of the school to write a Latin letter to the judges asking for a half-holiday during the Assizes.

[2] Extracts published in the *Monmothian*, Dec. 1933 and March 1934.

[3] W.M. Warlow, *A History of the Charities of William Jones at Monmouth and Newland*, (Bristol, 1899), 132.

[4] *Ibid.*, 137.

[5] St. Mary's, Monmouth, churchwardens' accounts 1706-1724.

[6] SVB. 3/3/1841.

[7] SVB. 5/3/1844.

[8] GL Ms. 15842/3 pp.380/381.

3 THE EIGHTEENTH CENTURY: 1714 - 1800

In 1706 the charitable monopoly that the school had enjoyed since its foundation was broken by the Society for the Promotion of Christian Knowledge opening a school at Overmonnow. There had been a Welsh Trust school since 1675, but it was concerned mainly with Welsh children and was designed to teach them English and so make them, 'more serviceable to their Country and to live more profitably in the World'. The SPCK schools were designed to teach children to read and write and to understand the church catechism.

The man behind them in Monmouth was the vicar, Herbert Pye. He was involved in the printing of the Bible in Welsh and had established a library in Overmonnow. He had also crossed swords with the lecturer, Charles Herbert, over his failure to control the behaviour of the inmates of the almshouses. So when the vicar set up his school, the lecturer 'publicly reproached' the whole idea of charity schools. His attack was reported to Henry Newman, the SPCK secretary in London, who replied that he hoped the author of 'this unchristian reflection, whoever he be, will live to be convinced that they are the best friends of Religion in general, and to the Church of England in particular, who wish all to be taught from the greatest to the least'.[1]

The local school was divided into four classes, the first learning the rudiments of reading and spelling, the second read the Psalter and New Testament, the third were taught to write, while in the fourth the boys did arithmetic, agriculture and navigation, and the girls spinning, knitting, weaving and plain needlework. The SPCK schools were supported by the local gentry who were happy to have better educated servants, but there was a minority on the lecturer's side who thought it dangerous to educate the poor above their station. So by the beginning of the century Monmouth School no longer considered itself a charity school.

Charles Herbert's time was troubled. In 1710 he and his sister were accused of 'detaining the mort money from the indigent persons' and a year later the almspeople were complaining that their pay was in arrear.[2] Mr. Bassett had died in 1713, and the usher had been in office for nineteen years. The new headmaster, Andrew Cuthbert, was therefore faced with a fairly stagnant situation. He was also new to a town which had passed through a turbulent period, with a ruling oligarchy of magistrates, clergymen and select burgesses tending to be jealous of any interference by the company with the running of the school and the selection of candidates for the almshouses. Moreover, financial problems in London affected the maintenance of the school buildings, made visitations from the wardens rarer, and control less effective. This made life more difficult for the headmaster who after ten years was glad to obtain the lectureship. Before that happened, he too had presented the school with a bell, proudly inscribed ANDREAS CUTHBERT ARCHIDIDASCALUS EE 1716. It was made by Evan Evans of Chepstow.

Attempts were made to control financial affairs by the appointment of a receiver, but the Monmouth charity's troubles stemmed from the curious way in which much of the property on which it depended was let on long leases, sometimes as much as 150 years. It was not until 1760 that the income was stabilised, and in the meantime few repairs took place amongst the school buildings.

Lack of these facilities, coupled with delay in paying staff and the almspeople, led to criticism of the sums spent in London on such luxuries as civic dinners. An example quoted was the St. Katherine's feast in 1731 when the tables were laden with one fish dish, twelve dishes of oysters and herbs, four venison pasties, nine turkeys, eight marrow puddings, eight dishes of tongue and udders, eight dishes of mince pies, ten dishes of boar and nine of custards. The second course included one dish of wildfowl, eleven of ducks and larks and nine of apple pies, as well as red and white wine and sack.[3] Such a weight of food was compared in Monmouth with the fare at the almshouses.

Throughout these difficult years, Andrew Cuthbert used his new broom with vigour, and when he became lecturer in 1723 he was praised for raising the numbers and increasing the school's reputation. James Birt, the usher succeeded him, and a Londoner, George Gwyn, in poor health but with the reputation of being the writer of risky ballads, became usher.

It had become customary for the staff to be appointed for one year only and to have to re-apply each year. The company maintained that fear of dismissal kept them up to scratch, whereas the staff claimed that they lacked security. As a result in 1730, lecturer, headmaster and usher united in protest and refused to re-apply. Their stand was considered in London and in 1732 they were all re-elected.

James Birt, who was not a great success, died in 1738 and Baynham Barnes, who had been usher since 1731, became headmaster. As he was already vicar of Dixton and Rockfield, he spent much of his time collecting his tithe and balancing his accounts. When he was not doing that he was converting the King's Chapel at Wyesham into a vicarage. Mr. Barnes might argue that all this outside activity was necessary because of his arrears in pay. One of his typically obsequious letters to the company, when he was usher in 1735, ran:

> Sir,
>   I have directed a bill as usual at ye season for half a year's salary due at midsummer last, and as there is a year due I hope it will meete with a ready acceptance.
>   I am, Sir, with all due respect to my much esteemed benefactors, ye gentlemen of ye worshipful company and yrself,
>   Your very much obliged
>   Humble Servant
>   B.Barnes.

As a result of Mr. Barnes's parochial activities, his successor as usher, John Thomas, ran the school single handed, and his letters to London are confident in his ability to restore it to its rightful position.

As usual in Monmouth there were other opinions, and a letter reached the company stating that since Mr. Cuthbert's time the school had declined so fast that parents were paying to send their children elsewhere. Although the usher continued to trumpet his achievements in having between fifty and sixty scholars, the company decided to check his facts and as a result of what they discovered wrote to the mayor and others 'to enquire how and by what means the Scholars in the School came to be reduced to so low a number as three ... whether it is owing to the Conduct and Behaviour of the present Master and Usher or any other Person'.

The sad state of the school was confirmed by the Reverend William Cole in 1743. After admiring the buildings, he wrote, 'Yet ye School which used to be very flourishing for all this part of the country, goes as I was informed, to decay'.[4]

A further enquiry was made about the usher, Mr. Thomas, 'whether he had attended the School every day ... how many hours a day and whether he had not been absent for weeks and months together in Bristol and London'. The company does not appear to have been aware that the usher had been suspended, and that they had told Francis Hollings to take his place. If anyone was to blame for reducing the numbers to three it was Mr. Barnes, and as if in recognition of this Mr. Thomas was taken back. In 1758 Mr. Barnes died, bequeathing a simple communion cup and salver to Dixton Church and his library to the school.

Although he had little time for teaching, that library included *An Essay on the*

Education of Youth in Grammar Schools (in which the vulgar method is examined and a new one proposed) by John Clark, 1730; and *An Essay to Facilitate the Education Of Youth by bringing down the Rudiments of Grammar to the Sense of Seeing which ought to be SINCRISIS fitted to the Children's Capacities for Learning, especially of the English, Latin and Greek Tongues* by M. Lewis, 1674.

He was succeeded by the Reverend John Crowe, a man who was most unlikely to restore the school to its former reputation, though he was going to remain at his post for twenty-one years. The continuing stagnation seems to have been unnoticed by the company until the lecturer informed them that the usher was teaching twenty-five boys and the headmaster only two. The usher then resigned and twelve boys left, so the school numbers fell to fifteen. One of the few during these years was Thomas Garnons who, in July 1762, copied out for his father the school rules in Latin.[5]

It is difficult to know what else he might have learned in the 1760s because the headmaster was continually at odds with his usher, had converted the playground into a field for his horse, had lost many of the library books, had forbidden the boys their favourite diversion of Fives (one of the oldest games played at the school) and had thrown away money on unsatisfactory repairs to the school buildings. Monmouth opinion was strongly against him, maintaining that 'he was naturally of so Morose Tyrannic Disposition and in fact so much the School Master it was impossible an Usher of any Ability or Evenness of Temper would ever agree to Conduct the School amicably with him'.

By 1779 it was obvious that it was not only Mr. Crowe's 'infirmity of body and mind' that was the trouble, he had gone completely mad. The company decided to make a visitation and appointed the Reverend Thomas Prosser as usher, 'to take the whole charge of the School' until a new headmaster was appointed.

He had plenty of problems to face. Roynon Jones, the lecturer, had died in 1773 and the Reverend George Smyth took his place. Unfortunately Mr. Jones's widow refused to move out of the house. Eventually she left, protesting that her husband had spent £200 on the building, and Mr. Smyth moved in, only to have to make a hurried escape when the roof fell on him. The clerk congratulated him on his good fortune and assured him that Mrs. Jones would soon put things right. She did not. So he asked to be allowed to rent lodgings until it was repaired. He estimated it would cost £400.

As nothing happened, he asked for permission to go abroad for a few months, but this was firmly refused. He waited until Autumn, the house continuing to collapse,

The School Laws at Monmouth

Deus imprimis colitor. Preces cum devoto animi affectu peraguntor. oculi non vagantor. Silentium esto. Nil profanum Legitor. In Schola diligentia quisque utitor. Submisse Loquitor tecum. Clare ad Praeceptorem. Nemini molestus esto orthographice Scribito. Arma Scholastica in promptu Semper habeto. Modestiam prae. Se omnes ferunto. vultus Gestus Incessus Componun= tor. Ajurgiis, pugnis, furtis, mendaciis, Juramentis et imprecationibus quisque abhorreto. Patrium Sermones fugito : Latinum exerce. vestis nec immunda Sit, Nec lacerata Caesaries Sit compta. Facies manusque Sint mundae. Diebus Dominicijs ad Templum bini Suo ordine omnes Incedunto Christianae Religionis Elementa Inferiores anglice, Superiores Latine Grae ce reddunto.. ♯ ♯ ♯ ♯ ♯ ♯ ♯ ♯ ♯ ♯ ♯ ♯ ♯ ♯ ♯ ♯

Qui Leges Violat, Piaculum esto

And · I am Your Dutiful Son

Tho.ˢ ✠ Garnons July y.ᵉ 7ᵗʰ 1762

The school laws, sent by Thomas Garnons to his father, 1762

The school laws (translation)

First above all else, let God be worshipped; let prayers be offered with devotion; let the eye not wander; let silence reign; let nothing profane be spoken; everyone in the school must work hard; let everyone speak softly to himself but clearly to his teacher. Let him not be a nuisance to anyone and write legibly; let him always have his school implements ready. Let everyone be modest; let his expressions, gestures and gait be composed. Let there be no quarrelling, fighting, thieving, lying, swearing and cursing. Let him avoid his native speech and use Latin. Clothes must be kept clean and hair combed and smooth. Faces and hands must be clean. On the Lord's Day everyone must go to Church, two by two in 'crocodile' to repeat the principles of the Christian religion, the younger ones in English, the older ones in Latin or Greek.

Whoever violates these rules, let him be punished.

and applied again to be allowed to go to France. The company agreed provided that someone performed his duties. This was arranged and he left. Two months later he applied for an extension and the company, which seemed unaware that he was still abroad, ordered him home.

He returned to find that Mrs. Jones was still refusing to pay, so both parties appealed to Chancery, which decided that as there was a balance in the funds, the house should be completely rebuilt by the charity. In 1778 Benjamin Maddox, whose sons gave Monmouth some of its finest buildings, was commissioned to rebuild. His estimate was £500, and when it was accepted he embarked on the project with speed and enthusiasm. The company seems to have been slow in coming to watch what was happening, and when a deputation did make the journey, they were horrified at the scale of the works. These included a huge garden with gazebo and ha-ha, more appropriate to an archbishop than a humble lecturer. They thought the old house could have been repaired for about £200. What was more, the final bill was £66 14s 9d greater than the estimate.

One of the reasons for the parlous condition of many Monmouth houses was the attempt by their owners, from the Duke of Beaufort downwards, to get rich by digging and selling 'cinders'. These were the refuse from Roman and medieval forges, which had provided useful foundations for the older buildings, and still contained iron. This could be extracted by efficient modern forges at Osbaston and down the Wye Valley, and most industrialists were willing to pay handsomely for them. As a result Monmouth, in the eighteenth century, suffered an orgy of destruction; most of the town walls which were built on cinders came down, Cinderhill Street lost its hill, islands in the river were removed, and in 1728, to the alarm of the company, the wall of the lecturer's garden fell down. An angry letter from the clerk to the mayor demanded reparation:

'It having been represented to the Master Wardens and Court of Assistants of this Company, that you have dug a peice of Ground at Monmouth,
carried away the Soil and made great profit from it, and in Consequence
of your digging there, part of the Wall belonging to the Lecturers Garden
is actually fallen down, and the rest very much weakened, I am directed
to acquaint you, that the Company not only expect, that the Wall shd
forthwith be rebuilt in a substantial and durable manner, but they also
desire to know, by what Right and Title, you have dug up that ground and
carried away the Soil, for as it is a Peice of Ground, which lies between
the Wall of the Lecturers house and another Peice of Ground, which
formerly belonged to the Company, and aftwds sold by them, they
apprehend the Property in this Intermediate Peice of Ground remained in

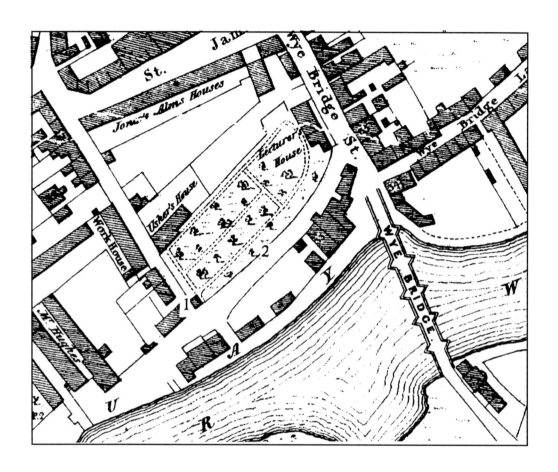

Plan of the lecturer's garden, 1835.
1. The gazebo, 2. the ha-ha

them.

As they are the Governours and Guardians of that Charity, its incumbent on them to see that no Injury is done to it and unless you can show an undoubted Right to do, what you have done there, they will demand of you an account of the Produce of what you have carried away and Satisfaction for it.

In Expectation of your Speedy and Satisfactory Answer hereto

  I am

        Gentlemen

            Your Mt: Obedt: hble Servt.

                Fotherly Baker'.[6]

After a long and angry exchange of letters, the council rebuilt the wall, protesting that it had been unstable anyway.

During Mr. Crowe's chaotic reign there seems to have been a succession of ushers, one of whom, Thomas Boaman alias Bowen, distinguished himself by leading a gang of boatmen and labourers in an attack on a service being held in Inch Lane (Worcester Street) by a group of Protestant dissenters. The gang broke in and then 'made a great noise and disturbance by shouting laughing whistling stamping of feet cursing and swearing and thereby disquieted the sd congregation to evil example and misused the Reverend John Broadbent, the Teacher of the sd Congregation'. A true bill was found against them and Mr. Bowen disappears from the records.[7]

The sad state of many schools was becoming obvious. William Cowper published *Tirocinium, or a Review of Schools* in 1784. He had enjoyed his time at Westminster but realised how much of it had been wasted and how much he would have gained by being taught at home. His poem is addressed to parents:

> 'Would you your son should be a sot or dunce,
> Lascivious, headstrong, or all these at once ?
>
> Train him in public with a mob of boys
> Childish in Mischief only and in noise'.

He did not blame the teachers:

> 'I blame not those who with what care they can
> Oerwatch the numerous and unruly clan'.

40

But parents should know what was happening:

> 'And seems it nothing in a father's eye
> That unimproved those many moments fly ?
> And is he well content his son should find
> No nourishment to feed his growing mind,
> But conjugated verbs and nouns declined ?'

Only a tutor in a boy's home would provide the answer:

> 'Are such men rare ? Perhaps they would abound
> Were occupation easier to be found,
> Were education, else so sure to fail,
> Conducted on a manageable scale,
> And schools that have outlived all just esteem,
> Exchanged for the secured domestic scheme'.

Cowper's pleasantly impracticable fantasy was unlikely to be welcomed by the average Monmouth parent.

Meanwhile Thomas Prosser continued to manage the school until a new headmaster was appointed. When the election arose he obtained the post. After that he never looked back, becoming lecturer in 1793, a member of the common council in 1802, vicar of Monmouth in 1815 and mayor and chief magistrate in 1806, 1813, 1816 and 1818. He was the first master from the school to become mayor. He was succeeded as usher by the Reverend John Powell who also rose, though less ambitiously, to be headmaster, lecturer, and curate of Dixton, Monmouth, Raglan and Llandenny.

The great variation in the number of boys attending the school in the eighteenth century was not peculiar to Monmouth. Winchester had the same problem over its fee paying boys: thirty-five in 1724, 123 in 1734, ten in 1750, 105 in 1779, and back to thirty-five in 1788.[8] Almost everything in those days depended on local opinion of the headmaster, and in a small, close-knit community like Monmouth there were plenty of people of the middle sort, 'watching from behind the Curtaine', to report on whether it was worth the entrance fee.

In the year that Mr. Prosser became lecturer a committee of the company decided that it would be proper for the usher to teach writing and arithmetic. There had for long been agitation in the town for the appointment of a writing master, and on the recommendation of Powell and Prosser, a friend of theirs, the Reverend Thomas Hughes of Christ Church, Oxford was appointed usher, with responsibility for these subjects.

Mr. Powell became headmaster after dedicating a book of 'Poems on Various Subjects' to the Haberdashers, whose 'munificence and candour' he had often experienced. In a disarming preface he admitted that what made him 'publish his effusions to the World (was) a desire for Fame - that illusive airy Phantom'.[9] Having satisfied his literary ambitions, he took the school in hand and, concentrating on boarders, quickly raised their numbers from forty-eight in 1798 to sixty-four in 1802. Although this may have sounded satisfactory to the company, it soon caused trouble in Monmouth, because as well as cramming all those boarders into his not very large house, he had reduced the number of day boys to ten. According to the Monmouth opposition he did this by allowing his boarders to bully the day boys until they were afraid to come to school. He was in fact running a private academy very similar to those springing up around him.

Sixty-eight inhabitants complained to the company in 1810 and the clerk was asked to write to the headmaster telling him that the school was still a free school and that he should not charge more than sixpence and two shillings for admission. He was in fact charging ten shillings and sixpence 'if not more'. He was also advertising widely:

The Reverend John Powell, M.A.
Master of the Grammar School, Monmouth
Boards and educates young Gentlemen on the following terms:
Board and Classical Tuition per annum   £20: 0: 0
Entrance   £1: 1: 0
Writing and Arithmetic per quarter   7: 6
Washing and mending socks per do   8: 6
N.B. Drawing, Dancing and French taught by approved Masters. A
Quarter's Notice or a Quarter's Board required when any young
gentleman leaves the school.

Amongst those taking drawing were John and Thomas Tudor, both future exhibitors at the Royal Academy. They provided William Coxe with many of the illustrations for his *Historical Tour of Monmouthshire* (1801). He thanked them in the preface for vying 'with each other to do him service'.

MONMOUTH ACADEMY
Conducted by the Rev. J. Gosling
Terms

Board & English for young gentlemen under 9	..				..			£20
„	„	„	„	„	9-14 years		..	£25
„	„	„	„	„	over 14	..	..	£30
Greek & Latin languages with the Eton method ..						..		£3
Mathematics	..	..	..	..	..	..	..	£3
Geography ..	..	..	..	..	..	..	..	£2
French	..	..	..	..	..	..	..	£4
Drawing	..	..	..	..	..	..	..	£4

Entrance One Sovereign
Each young gentleman may have a separate bed

Monmouth Academy's terms *c*1830

Mathematics, Fortifications, Projections, Descriptive Geometry, Military Surveying, Levelling, Perspective, Hill Drawing, Practising from Drawings & Models, Drawing as taught in the schools of France and Prussia, also sketching from natural objects. Navigation is here taught with the utmost approved methods of keeping a Journal at sea, Meridian and double altitudes, Finding the Longitude by Chronometer and Lunar Observations etc. Complete courses in Geometry, Algebra, Differential and Integral Calculus, Plane and Spherical Trigonometry, and in such branches of Science as apply to the active pursuits of life. English Grammar, Composition, the Art of Reading Well, History, Geography etc. . . . Commercial Arithmetic and Book Keeping.
Mr. Lebert can adduce, if required, satisfactory testimonials from nearly all quarters.

Dixton Academy's syllabus *c*1837

Monmouth at this time was notorious for its lack of sanitation, and William Smith in his *Report on the State of Monmouth* in 1818 had pointed out that most of the town's drinking water came either from the rivers or from springs in the church-yard, percolating the graves to wells in the basements of the houses. As a result there had been outbreaks of 'putrid fever' in the almshouses. The lecturer believed he had cured this by having the houses whitewashed. But questions also arose when it was realised how many boys were crammed into the headmaster's house. Mr. Gosling, who ran a rival private classical academy, took advantage of this when advertising his sleeping arrangements. He was ahead of his time. Boys were still two to a bed at Rugby in 1894.[10]

The company was growing impatient with the school and demanded more information from the head. So Mr. Powell submitted a list of thirty-seven boys of whom twenty-two were boarders. He did not explain what had happened to the rest but gave details of the curriculum, stating that the top classes were learning Latin, Greek and little else, while the fourteen boys on the commercial side were being taught writing, merchant's accounts, geography and English grammar by a writing master charging three guineas a year. It compared unfavourably with the exotic prospectus for Mr. Lebert's academy at Dixton.

Mr. Lebert's military enthusiasm proved too much for his small staff and before long he moved elsewhere. But impatience with the purely classical bias of many grammar schools was widespread and Humphrey Repton, the landscape gardener-to-be, was removed from Norwich Grammar School because 'My father thought proper to put the stopper on the vial of classical literature, having determined to make me a rich, rather than a learned man'.[11]

There was another point of view, that wider education meant shallower education; and this idea was given publicity in the introduction to the report of the Clarendon Commission on the public schools in 1864. 'Among the services which the Public Schools have rendered is undoubtedly to be reckoned the maintenance of classical literature as the staple of English education, a service which far outweighs the error of having clung to these studies too exclusively'.[12] Indeed the standards of nineteenth century literature, scholarship and parliamentary debate have little to fear in comparison with those produced since the classical bias was reversed.

Although Mr. Powell had to endure much criticism from the town, he managed to produce several university candidates. One such was James Endell Tyler who went to Oriel, became a fellow, a tutor, and ultimately dean. He was a friend of Newman and in 1826 became rector of St. Giles in the Fields. In 1845 Sir Robert

Peel made him canon residentiary of St Paul's. He wrote many books, usually tracts against papal errors, such as *The Image-Worship of the Church of Rome proved to be contrary to Holy Scripture* (published in 1847 but the library copy still uncut). More readable, and well researched was an excellent two volume, *Henry of Monmouth: Memoirs of the Life and Character of Henry V*, published in 1838. In it he mentions playing when a boy in the castle where Henry was born.[13]

References

[1] Correspondence and minutes of the SPCK relating to Wales, 1699-1740.
[2] MBA. Council minutes, 1710-1711.
[3] Archer, *op. cit.* 132.
[4] BM. Additional Ms. 5811, fol.100.
[5] MBA. File Z.
[6] MBA. Schools.
[7] MBA. Quarter Session records, 25/1/1779.
[8] *A History of Winchester College*, 1899.
[9] Published Hereford, 1783.
[10] C. Dukes, *Health at School*, 1894.
[11] Quoted by Paul Langford, *A Polite and Commercial People*, (Oxford, 1989).
[12] The report was the basis of the Public Schools Act, 1868.
[13] For Tyler see Geoffrey Faber, *Oxford Apostles*, (Penguin, 1954).

James Endell Taylor by G. Clint, in the vestry of St. Giles-in-the-Fields, London

4 TROUBLE WITH THE TOWN: 1800 - 1859

Charles Heath described the schoolroom in 1804 as being twenty yards long and eight yards wide. There was a raised desk for the master at one end and a spacious gallery at the other where the boys were taught writing and accounts. He was more impressed by the staff quarters, especially the rebuilt lecturer's 'very desirable residence' with its extensive garden, enclosed by a high brick wall, and its fine gazebo overlooking the river. The master's house was also a 'modern-built brick mansion' with garden and playground at the back. Although the usher had a garden, 'yet the residence is very inferior to either of the former mansions'.[1] Maintenance continued to be a problem, and in 1816 it was stated that no repairs of any sort had been carried out in school or almshouses since 1793. Even so Nicholas Carlisle was impressed in 1818, especially with the lecturer's house and garden which seems to have taken up more than half of the two acres which the school covered.[2]

When the lecturer and headmaster became respectively vicar and curate of Monmouth in 1815, there must have been many occasions when parish duties kept both of them away from the school. This problem seems to have been overcome by Mr. Powell when headmaster. He hired a writing master to fill his place paying the man himself. The usher was presumably responsible for the rest of the school.

By 1818, when the lecturer was mayor for the fourth time, the school became involved in a long dispute over the election of the town councillors. Until the beginning of the century the council had been a self-perpetuating body, very much under the control of Monmouth's *eminence grise*, the Duke of Beaufort's agent. The rebellion against this comfortable establishment was led by a group of radical independent burgesses who demanded more influence over its affairs.

Amongst the radicals was Thomas Thackwell, 'Honest Tom' as he was called, who was to spend the next fifty years campaigning against the school on behalf of the town. To begin with he was effective because his complaints were rational. Remote control by a London company had always presented problems to both school and company, and Mr. Thackwell demanded the appointment of local visitors to control affairs. In 1825 nine establishment figures were appointed and presented with fine manuscript volumes describing the particulars of the charity. At their third meeting they discussed at length whether the statutes entitled the school 'to teach reading and writing or rather the very first elements of learning'.

A List of the Boys in Mr. Jones's Free Grammar School 1825.

	Boys	Books used
First Class	William Parry	Horace, Sallust, Greek Testament
Second	Charles Homfray	Virgil, Cæsar's Comm? Greek Testament
	William Monkhouse	
Third	Alfred Homfray	Ovids Epistles – Cor Nepos
	William Adams	
	Boarder – Under Mr Jones	
Fourth	Thomas Dubberly	Cor. Nepos. Delectus
Fifth	John Swift	
	William Homfray	
	John Williams	
	John Ford	
	Charles Parry	Latin Grammar
	Robert Price	
	John Monkhouse	
	Ebenezer Rogers	
	James Powell	Under Mr Prosser
Sixth	James Webb	
	Frederick Rees	Under Mr Jenkins – English only
	Charles Dowding	
	Edward Williams	

19

The boys as listed in 1825

They decided that 'this ambiguity had been fatal to the interests of the School'. A writing master must be appointed, to appear daily for one hour each morning and afternoon and teach arithmetic as well.[3] This was the first of the many attempts to teach writing which proved permanent.

The visitors conceded another of Thackwell's demands, that boys from outside the borough should only be admitted if the numbers had fallen below one hundred and there were no local boys capable or desirous of being admitted. William Jones, who had become headmaster in 1823, responded to these new decisions by admitting ninety-seven boys, many of whom could not read, and then resigning.[4]

Mr. Jones had been an unfortunate choice and his brutal use of the cane had led to complaints to the visitors. They reprimanded him and told him that the masters should abandon the cane and confine themselves to the rod, 'as used in public schools generally - the punishment to take place after the lessons were over, when it may be inflicted with more deliberation'.[5] They also wrote to the governors asking them not to appoint any more masters from the town 'owing to the party spirit which is supposed to prevail'.[6]

Flogging was a problem which was to continue throughout the century, but the locals were happy to compare Mr. Jones's behaviour with what the *Monmouthshire Merlin* reported was the treatment in neighbouring Newland. Here, in 1839, 'the old system of corporal punishment is in great measure abandoned, and is super-seded by that mutual confidence between master and pupil which inspires emulation in the young mind, and learning becomes a pleasure not a test'.[7]

More difficult for the visitors was the large influx of illiterate local boys which Mr. Jones had bequeathed to the school. They seem to have conducted a reading test which got rid of thirty-four of the intake, but they were still saddled with sixty-three whom they admitted and placed on a new school register.[8] Examinations were conducted by the visitors in future, but as it was confined to reading, and no account was taken of age nor how many times the boy sat, it was difficult not to get into the school in the long run. It emerged later that the page they had to read was always the same page and from the same book. So it became possible for cunning parents to teach the known page by heart, thus enabling their offspring to pass without even looking at the book.

When Mr. Jones departed in 1828, the Reverend John Oakley Hill was appointed head, his brother Benjamin Hill writing master and George Nesham usher. All were on six months' probation. The usher was soon found to be unfit as he failed to read a few pages of Caesar[9] so Benjamin Hill took his place, and a Mr. Baker

The old school and almshouses by Benjamin Hill, Usher, 1829

became writing master. It proved too much for him: he died within a few months[10] to be followed by John Hyam, a member of an old Monmouth family. John Powell, the lecturer, died penniless at the age of 76 in 1836, and was replaced by the Reverend James Crowther.

One of the continuing problems was accommodation. In 1833 the upper school was taught classics 'in a small slip or upstairs gallery, boarded off at one end of the Schoolroom, very confined and inconvenient in itself, and very injurious to the appearance of the School. The Headmaster when shut up in this closet cannot see what is going on in the Lower School'.[11] More usually masters taught vast numbers of boys in large rooms; Dr. Keate at Eton was at one time taking a form of nearly 200 boys.

When Queen Victoria came to the throne, Monmouth's first infant school was founded. A collection was taken at the local coronation service and with the proceeds a house in St. Mary's Street (Mr. Wigmore's) was bought. A new front was placed on it in an attempt to imitate the old schoolroom of 1614. But in other streets, rival academies were sprouting fast, many of them offering subjects which were still spurned at Monmouth School.

The academy opened by Mr. Lebert in the Dixton Road probably offered the widest choice, but there had been a fashionable Young Ladies' Boarding Academy at Great Castle House since about 1770 graced (*inter alia*) by the children of the Persian mistress of Sir Harford Jones Brydges, first British Ambassador to Persia. This was over 100 years before the High School was founded. There was also a Catholic seminary in St. Mary's Street, (in which the future Cardinal Vaughan was a boy), a classical academy in Whitecross Street, the Rosebrook Cottage seminary at Dixton, the May Hill academy, facing the school from across the river, several dame schools in Monk Street and Monnow Street, and Monsieur Adolphe in Agincourt Square offering to teach penmanship to young ladies and gentlemen between the ages of 12 and 70.[12] Nobody taught Welsh in spite of an impassioned appeal for a Welsh academy, 'For I am convinced that many would avail themselves of the opportunity of learning so beautiful a language'.[13]

This rash of new schools had two consequences; it gave added power to Mr. Thackwell's demand for change at the school, and it finally convinced the company that there must be a relaxation of the classical bias of the charity if it was to regain its unique position in the town. Such changes came to light slowly in a series of statutes published in 1828, 1847, and 1854. During the same period control over the company's expenditure passed from the Court of Chancery to the Charity Commissioners. This last-named body was to prove yet another target for those, like Mr. Thackwell, seeking greater local control of the school.

Complaints from parents were usually dismissed by the visitors as frivolous. Their general attitude was that of a later headmaster of Marlborough, who thought parents were the very last people who should be allowed to have children. But in 1840 they made two concessions: that there should be a fire in the schoolroom and that the playground should be drained. Occasional complaints if made direct to the governors received consideration, as did a letter from two parents in 1840. The governors referred their letter back to the visitors who dealt with it in detail. There were fourteen complaints, considered by the visitors one by one.

1. That the rules of the school had not been given to the parents when their boys were admitted. The visitors found that this was not the master's fault.

2. That there was no school on Saturday. The master claimed to have had permission to abolish it, but the visitors thought that attendance on Saturday morning should be enforced.

3. That the length of the vacations was excessive. The visitors agreed to limit them to thirty-five days at midsummer and twenty-eight at Christmas.

4. That the master was often absent. The visitors agreed that no engagement should interfere with his attendance at school.

5. That the scripture reading at night had been abandoned. The visitors deplored this but rejoiced that the master had recently revived it.

6. That catechizing did not take place and the master and usher did not accompany the boys to church. The visitors ordered that catechizing should continue and that the writing master should accompany the boys to church if the master and usher were absent.

7. That geo (*sic*) globes and mathematics were not taught. The visitors acquitted the staff of all blame.

8. That not enough time was devoted to writing and ciphering. The visitors thought the writing master was not to blame.

9. That the usher chastised at the time the fault was committed. The visitors regretted this, forbade it in future, and ordered the rod to be used rather than the cane.

10. That the parents of two boys were paying for extra instruction. The visitors could see nothing wrong in this provided it did not interfere with the running of the school.

11. That Thomas and Trevor Williams, sons of one of the complainants, had been given undue and useless punishment in being sent to Coventry and being given excessive tasks to prepare at home. The visitors found the second master blameless.

12. On the suspension of these two boys, the visitors were surprised that the master

had not told them as they would then have expelled them.

13. The other parent's complaint was considered frivolous, and his conduct to the master exceedingly insolent and improper.

14. Finally the visitors agreed to provide all boys and parents with an amended copy of the school rules.[14]

A request that there should be a pump for the boys in the playground was dismissed as too expensive, and it took many years for the pump to arrive. Where the day boys washed is not clear. Hygiene was not a priority. There was no bath at Charterhouse until 1903. Instead, boys were advised to have a good wash on the last day of the holidays and again when they got home thirteen weeks later.[15] Darkness helped to hide grime and the town complained bitterly that the school had not spent more than six guineas a year on Monmouth gas.[16]

Another factor affecting the attitude of outsiders to the school was the introduction of the new provincial newspapers. Previously, what was going on was made public by unreliable rumours. But with the advent of the *Monmouthshire Merlin* and the *Monmouthshire Beacon*, these two new sources of information, often just as unreliable, made such information more widely available. From its early days the *Merlin* adopted an avuncular approach, pontificating on how 'a perpetual charity ... coeval with the existence of Great Britain as a civilised country', could be threatened by barbarians daring 'to confiscate the inheritance of the poor'.[17] Naturally, Mr. Thackwell made much of this fresh approach.

The Court of Chancery had often been as critical as the locals, and in 1827 made a visitation in which the members reported unpleasantly that 'The present Masters, though so liberally paid, and having so little to do, consider themselves engaged only to teach Latin and Greek. A school teaching those branches of learning only will never be useful to a place of such confined population as Monmouth'. At the same time it was expected that the writing master should include in his timetable a wider range of subjects which were to include English grammar, geography, the use of globes, algebra, decimals and the first principles of mathematics. The headmaster was to confine himself to English, Latin, Greek, geography and mathematics.

Three years before this visitation the *Westminster Review* had said much the same: 'from six to eight, till sixteen or seventeen, nine or ten months in every precious year of youth are occupied, for 6 to 8 hours every day, in learning or trying to learn, a little Latin and less Greek; in attempting in fact, not to read and understand the matter of a classical author ... but the grammar, the syntax, the parsing, the quantities and the accents; not in learning to write and speak the languages, but of getting by rote a few scraps of poetry ... in ten years of this labour, privation, punishment, slavery and expense, what is gained even of this useless trash? Nothing'.[18]

The problem of matching the school curriculum to the average intake can be seen if one lists the occupations of the parents of all boys admitted in 1833 and 1834. There were: nine farmers, five forgemen, five labourers, four masons, four carpenters, four bakers, four innkeepers, four widows, three shoemakers, three shopkeepers, two saddlers, two coachmen and one hatter, miller, cooper, grocer, clockmaker, constable, gatekeeper, turnkey, clerk, smith, tiler, soldier, butcher, and widower; leavened or otherwise, by two solicitors and two gentlemen. R.R. Webb, first Smith's prizeman and senior wrangler, came of good Herefordshire farming stock.[19]

The 1847 statutes went into great detail, and along with those of 1854 and 1868, are published in full in Warlow.[20] They stated that candidates for admission should receive instructions from the headmaster at least ten days before they were examined by the visitors; the school day was to be from 7.30 to 5 in summer and 9 to 4.30 in winter; physical science, book keeping and drawing were added to the subjects available; parents could apply for their boys to attend worship at denominations other than C. of E.; up to twelve book prizes could be awarded at each half-yearly examination by the visitors; certain boys, approved by the Master, might use the library at certain times, 'No personal chastisement is ... to take place at the time of committing the faults, but on the following morning'; no master should take boarders or any gratuity from parents or boys; and those members of the staff in school houses were to keep them water-tight and repair all defective glazing, tiling, slating and walls at their own expense.

The statutes of 1854 divided the school into Upper Classical and Lower Commercial and opened the entrance to day boys from Gloucestershire, Herefordshire and Monmouthshire. This was a compromise between two petitions, one from the vicar and eighty-one inhabitants asking that fee-paying boarders be allowed, and one from the mayor and 500 inhabitants asking that all the old restrictions remain.

But while the statutes could be revised, visitors issue commands, and Mr. Thackwell and his friends complain, it was for the headmaster to keep the school going. Often all three bodies were ignored. Mr. Thackwell could hold meetings at which Mr. Dubberley, claiming to be the first free boy to be admitted, described in detail how, in 1823, he had been 'tasked to an immoderate extent - flogged for speaking to any boarder - and otherwise treated with the greatest indignity'. Mr.

Swift, many times mayor, could tell that in his day, when there were seventy to eighty boarders, he and his brother had been flogged every day.[21] But headmasters had to keep order. This, too, led to trouble.

Mr. Watherston, who had become headmaster in 1844, after a few months as a curate in Marylebone, took little notice of the rule that chastisement should not take place at the time the fault was committed. In 1852 he was taken to court by H.G. Alpass, one of his own boys, who told the court that he had been taken to the headmaster by Mr. Thompson for not doing his imposition, writing out the six tenses of *esse* four times. Mr. Watherston told him to hold out his hand; he said 'No Sir'. The head said it again and he still refused. He was then struck repeatedly on the head and shoulders and driven from the room. The head was represented by a solicitor who described with relish how, in his schooldays, he had seen a boy felled by a blow from an usher, and that it was normal to birch a boy till blood fell upon the floor. If a head could not use a gentle caning such as Alpass had received, he might as well retire. He then called a boy named Davies who said that Alpass had received a normal punishment, adding unctuously that no boy in such cases should use his own judgement.[22] But a reaction was setting in and in 1853 *The Times* was shocked by the story of the beating of the Earl of Galloway's son at Eton and the breaking of five sticks on the shoulders of a boy at Winchester.

The Alpass case was dismissed; what happened to Davies when he got back to school is not known, but even the opposition was alarmed at the thought of a boy suing the head and Mr. Cossens, the postmaster, wrote an anxious letter to the local paper asking boys to complain to the visitors first.[23] Mr. Thackwell, now over seventy, had passed the baton to Mr. Cossens and retired from the fray after receiving an engraved salver and being thanked for 'locking the stable door before the steed was stolen'. The salver was inscribed:

PRESENTED
on 31st July 1844 to
MR. THOMAS THACKWELL
by the inhabitants of Monmouth
with a tea and coffee service
as a tribute of gratitude for his
Unwearied and Successful Exertions in Restoring
the
FREE GRAMMAR SCHOOL
in that Town to the Original Purpose
of its benevolent founder
WILLIAM JONES.[24]

In 1850 the visitors agreed to appoint a paid examiner and E.H. Bradbury of Balliol came to the school in the following year. He received something of a shock; Greek was taught only to three boys, two of them indifferently; Divinity was the largest subject, but as all boys copied from one another he was unable to judge, and there was even more copying under the writing master. As far as he could see, the standard was not high for a school sending boys to a university. This was due to the class of boys admitted, with no suitable home background or previous education. He found only eight boys deserving and painstaking. The rest were idle, lacking in intelligence and less well-informed than the upper boys of a good National School. This was partly due to most of the teaching being done by rote. His report six months later was no better: 'Decidedly a general want of improvement in the School'. This was shown by the fact that there were twenty vacancies and only five applicants.[25] Three years earlier there had been twenty applicants for three places.

In 1852 there was still no improvement: 'They knew nothing before and they know nothing or next to nothing now', he wrote; 'many of the boys appear so ignorant even of the Elements of Religion as to be a disgrace to their parents, still more than to their teachers'.[26] The head pleaded that classes should be limited to fifteen, and that entrance should be half-yearly rather than quarterly, but blamed the staff, especially Mr. Hyam, who was accustomed to leave a senior boy to teach his class while he attended to his business as a corn merchant in Monnow Street. He was paid £90 a year and Mr. Watherston thought he could get a good national schoolmaster capable of teaching 100 boys for £80. He was unsuccessful and Mr. Hyam hung on until 1860 when he was asked to retire on a pension and make way for someone 'with a more modern approach to teaching'.[27]

A new examiner, C.J. Homfrey, repeated in 1853 that the school's many benefits would only be felt when the boys came better prepared to receive them. Under his guidance there was an improvement; Dictation and formal spelling had been introduced, Tate's *Geometry* 'which shows the practical application in the ordinary course of life of the principles of Arithmetic' was recommended; and by 1856 poetry was being taught, 'though repeated with little regard to meaning or punctuation'. A year later a new examiner praised the new entry's 'strict accuracy in elementary teaching - the only good foundation of all that is valuable in school'.[28] By then there were thirty-six applicants for eight vacancies.

Examiners were occasionally surprised by a boy like Charles Parson, 'in a class by himself, who in half a year (1848) read part of the *Odyssey*, four books of Herodotus, the *Antigone* of Sophocles, four books of Livy and the whole of Terence ... and showed diligence and accuracy when examined in each ... a lad of considerable polish'.[29]

Speech days began in the 1850s and were often combined with the examination of new entrants, and a floral display. In 1857, for instance, when the guests arrived they found the schoolroom decorated 'with flowers in wreaths, garlands and elegant devices ... entirely executed by the Scholars themselves'. The report of the examiner was then read, praising the school, but deploring the early age at which boys left. Books were awarded as prizes, and amongst the titles were *Robinson Crusoe*, *Recreations in Physical Geography*, Layard's *Nineveh*, Cowper's poems, Burton's *History of the Church*, and *The History of Sandford and Merton for Juvenile Britons*. The last-named, by Thomas Day, was timely, as it described the effect of good teaching on the rich, unpleasant Tommy Merton (boarder) who is compared with the upright but poor Harry Sandford (free boy).

After the prize-giving, candidates for three places were examined by being asked to read a passage from *The History of England*. The chairman of the visitors announced that the winners were two Monmouth boys and one from Coleford. Immediately a member of the audience, J.G. George, a solicitor, rose and asked why a Monmouth boy amongst the candidates had been rejected. The chairman pacified him and replied that only when boys were equally eligible should a town boy be preferred. If Mr. George thought otherwise he should go to law.[30]

The adjutant of the local militia, Captain Carter, then changed the line of attack in a series of very long letters extolling Pate's Grammar School at Cheltenham which he said should be the model for Monmouth to follow.[31] This aroused a certain amount of local resentment and another correspondent, Paterfamilias, turned his attention to the conditions in which the staff had to teach: a barn-like building in which 100 boys were taught simultaneously by three teachers. More apparatus, blackboards, maps, globes and books were necessary as were better desks. Why, he asked, did so few local boys go on to higher education? and gave as the answer the fact that 'no foreign language was taught, no drawing, little mathematics nor any of the ordinary problems of Land Survey, Gauging or Navigation - not to mention Astronomy, Gunnery and other branches of study'. He ended his letter by blaming apathy and lack of foresight amongst the people of Monmouth, always harking back to William Jones and ignoring current problems such as gauging and gunnery.[32]

Mr. Watherston was well aware of the difficulties and had written a long letter to the governors in 1852 describing the folly of starting boys on Latin and Greek before they could speak English. He was being forced to provide 'a course which has secured to the recipient of it a smattering of a dead language, in the majority of cases tending to nauseate and repel the mind from books hereafter ... a sacrifice of youthful time which might have been employed as a seed time for a more prosperous harvest'.[33]

In this he was backed by C.J. Homfrey who, in 1855, traced the problems of the school back to the parents, 'many of whom think that a child is educated because it is sent to a school for a few hours daily', and who 'value education only for the pecuniary benefits it may be expected to produce'.[34] Such parents took their children away far too early.[35] Meanwhile the headmaster, plagued by directives from visitors and governors, was being told to teach French without anyone to teach it[36] and instructed to obtain good teachers without the money to attract them.

But twenty years later George Trevelyan complained of the time wasted in school by boys, of an age when their grandfathers were fighting in the Peninsula, dividing the day between Latin verse, their cricket scores and the tuck shop.

He was also having to face more general criticism of the public schools from the literary world. Mary Wollstonecraft in *The Vindication of the Rights of Women* considered such schools 'hot-beds of Vice and folly ... the relaxation of the junior boys is Mischief, of the seniors Vice'. Sidney Smith, remembering his days at Winchester, considered the public school system an intense system of tyranny of which the English are very fond. 'They think it fits a boy for the world, but the world, bad as it is, has nothing half so bad'.

Macaulay was not likely to make it any easier for Mr. Watherston to find good teachers when in one of his more unbalanced denunciations in 1847 he described them as 'the refuse of other callings - discarded servants or ruined tradesmen; who cannot do a sum of three; who would not be able to write a common letter; who do not know whether the earth is a cube or a sphere, and cannot tell whether Jerusalem is in Asia or America'.

Mr. Watherston withstood the criticism for a time but abandoned the struggle in 1859 and became the lecturer. In so doing he seems to have forsaken the world, selling his carpets, his books and his curtains, to say nothing of a large collection of casks and barrels and '19 dozen choice Bordeaux St. Julien wine'.[37]

References

[1] C. Heath, *Historical and Descriptive Account ... of the Town of Monmouth*, (Monmouth, 1804).

[2] N. Carlisle, *A Concise Description of Endowed Grammar Schools in England and Wales*, 1818, II, 73.

[3] SVB. 16/4/1825, 3/8/1825.

[4] SVB. 22/3/1828.

[5] SVB. 12/12/1827.

[6] SVB. 5/6/1829.

[7] MM. 13/7/1839.

[8] SVB. 18/7/1828.

[9] SVB. 10/10/1828.

[10] SVB. 4/9/1829.

[11] Report of the Commissioners for Inquiring Concerning Charities (1819-1837), 439. Monmouth included in England in this report.

[12] Kissack, *Monmouth: the Making of a County Town*, (Phillimore, 1975), 141-148.

[13] MM. 10/11/1838.

[14] SVB. 18/12/1839, 2/9/1840.

[15] L.F. Bushell, *School Memories*, 1962, 41.

[16] MBA. Paving and Lighting, 1840.

[17] MM. 13/6/1829.

[18] Vol.I, 1823, 65.

[19] SVB. 1/3/1833.

[20] Warlow, *op. cit.*, 367-400.

[21] MB. 20/11/1852.

[22] SVB. 21/12/1852. Alpass was expelled a month later for bringing to an examination written answers to questions he expected to be asked.

[23] MB. 27/11/1852.

[24] MB. 27/7/1844. The salver is now in the Monmouth Museum. (His grandson Seabright was expelled four years later).

[25] SVB. 24/6/1851, 16/12/1851.

[26] SVB. 5/7/1852.

[27] SVB. 18/6/1860.

[28] SVB. 18/4/1856.

[29] SVB. 20/6/1848.

[30] MB. 20/6/1857.

[31] MB. 1/11/1856.

[32] MB. 12/2/1859, 19/2/1859.

[33] SVB. 22/3/1852.

[34] SVB. 24/12/1855.

[35] SVB. 15/6/1857.

[36] SVB. 6/12/1853.

[37] MB. 29/1/1859.

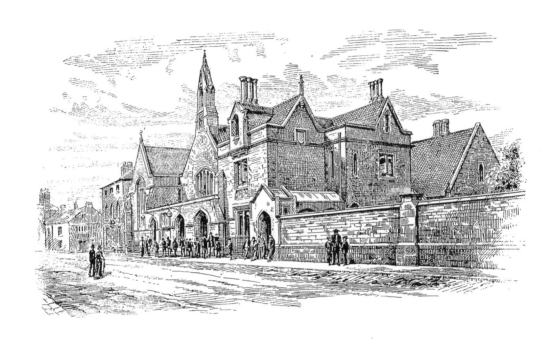

The school in 1865

5 C.M. ROBERTS: 1860 - 1891

Charles Manley Roberts, who became headmaster in 1859, was one of the few laymen to be appointed to this post. He was quickly ordained by the Bishop of Hereford and became curate of Whitchurch in 1861. He took over a school which had gone through difficult times, and was still hampered by the ban on boarders, by the dilapidated state of the buildings, and by the damage done to its reputation by the more outspoken critics in the local press. But he was a disciplinarian and H.P. Hale remembered in 1876, as one of the confirmation class which had to learn not only the Catechism but also the Thirty-Nine Articles, waiting tongue-tied while Mr. Roberts went to his cupboard murmuring 'A little interview with my persuader perhaps', and coming back caressing his cane.[1]

The low state of the school was addressed in an editorial in the *Monmouthshire Beacon* of 14 April 1860, entitled "India and Our Grammar School". 'India,' the editor wrote, 'till recently was shut against the great body of the youth of England'. Young men might go, yet without interest or patronage, they would be lost in corruption. 'But now India offers rank and wealth to the gifted, educated and enterprising young ... No ban or restriction shuts out the son of a tradesman or peasant, or the alumni of any educational establishment ... Why should not boys of ability in Monmouth and its neighbourhood be qualified ... to compete for these prizes ? ... The Haberdashers have taken little interest in Monmouth ... so it is imperative on the people, conscious of their rights, and feeling the importance of placing their children in an educational position to compete for Government appointments, to demand of the Haberdashers such an application of funds as shall raise the character and efficiency of the School'.

Sixty-four years later Lionel James was to repeat this plea when at speech day he complained that few boys entered the Colonial Service. He would like to see three out of four leavers go abroad. Far too many went into banks. It was as if the whole of the next generation was going to get a living looking after one anothers' bank accounts.[2] But in 1947 the Master of the Haberdashers stated that joining the Civil Service 'merely afforded ample opportunity for those who do not want to accept responsibility'.

Mr. Roberts was to remain headmaster for thirty-two years. He was to rebuild the school, abolish the limitation on one hundred boys, open the entrance examination to England and Wales, introduce new fees and scholarships, gain representation on the Headmasters' Conference, and admit boarders. It was not all plain sailing, and there was vociferous opposition in the Thackwell tradition to many of the changes he made, especially the problem of boarders. The main argument for accepting them was that, while they were forbidden, boys boarded in the town, often in disreputable lodgings where the staff had little control. Another argument in their favour was the claim, made by 'The Father of One of the Boys' in the *Beacon*, that before boarders were abolished they spent up to £5000 a year in the town. The same writer denounced those who jeered at boys wearing the new jockey cap with its black leather peak, and told them to go to Eton, Shrewsbury or Harrow, 'where caps are the distinguishing mark of the student'.[3] Mr. Watherston had introduced them because of unbecoming behaviour in the streets where there had been much ribald comment by town boys.[4]

Roberts was ably assisted by two members of the staff, William Pitt and William Roseveare. Examiners in the 1860s were to refer frequently to the excellence of the mathematical teaching and the impressive instruction boys were receiving in their own language. In 1862 L.B. Seeley wrote, 'If a commercial education is not to range beyond the mother tongue, then I will venture to say that in few institutions of this kind can such a training be obtained in greater perfection than at Monmouth'. He then praised the competence of the staff and concluded, 'I beg leave to congratulate you on the flourishing state of this well organised and well adminis-tered institution ... and on the benefits which the Monmouth Grammar School is made the means of conveying to the district in the centre of which it is situated'.[5]

Under Mr. Roberts the number of candidates for admission rose dramatically. At the same time the number of those admitted fell, possibly because the tests became harder:

Year	Candidates	Admissions
1859	35	35
1860	29	26
1861	45	34
1862	65	26
1863	85	26
1864	79	33
1865	99	23
1866	76	31
1867	126	18

This new evidence in the school's favour led some of those supporting boarders to respond in verse to the report of a public meeting in 1864 opposing them.[6]

Apropos to a Public Meeting held in the Borough Court of a County Town* in one of the most enlightened and flourishing parts of England, on Tuesday, Dec. 13th, 1864.

"*No Boarders!*" is the townsmen's talk ;
"*No Boarders!*" scrawls the urchin's chalk,
"*No Boarders!*" screams the truant boy,
Of Jones's School the pride and joy.
"*No Boarders!*" scowls a lawyer's frown,
And eke one Justice of our town ;
No customers our shops to fill,
And bring fresh money to the till ;
No hatters—for no hats we want,
Our money as our brains so scant !
"No tailors " shout the *sans culottes*—
No long-tail'd coats, no trim-made frock ;
" No boats " the boatmen fiercely cry,
To ply our craft on far-famed Wye ;
No Visitors our Inns t'uphold,
And turn our coppers into gold :
No strangers here to lodge and live,
And tow'rds our public wants to give ;
No " larning " fit to teach our betters,
And make us more than know our letters.
For " Latin," Greek, and lore " polite,"
We care not, or to read or write ;
No School beyond our A, B, C,
For this is School enough for " we."
No trade—no go—no progress—no !
As we've gone backwards, so we'll go ;
Our houses full of rust and rot,
Our tenants going, or gone to pot—
We want no more than what we've got.

Poem in support of boarders

Deputation of Haberdashers at the laying of the chapel foundation stone, 1864

.Constables.
Band of the Monmouth Rifle Volunteers,
The Scholars,
The Inhabitants of Jones's Almshouses,
Choristers,
MASTERS OF THE SCHOOL, VIZ.:
Mr. Earle, Writing Master.
Mr. Pitt, Second Master,   Mr. Roseveare, Third Master.
Rev. Charles M. Roberts, Head Master,
Leonard B. Seeley, Esq., the Examiner.
The Rev. John D. Watherstone, Lecturer.
The Architect (W. Snooks, Esq.) | The Contractor (Mr. Collins)
with Plans. | with Trowel.
Captain Bosanquet (Commandant of the Monmouth Volunteers),
with the Members of the Corps.
The Town Beadle with Mace.
The Town Clerk (T. J. A. Williams, Esq.)
The Members of the Town Council of Monmouth.
Treasurer of the Borough (W. A. Williams, Esq.)
ALDERMEN, VIZ.:
T. Watkins, Esq. | W. Williams, Esq.
John Powles, Esq. | Henry Gosling, Esq.
The Worshipful the Mayor.
CLERGY OF MONMOUTH, VIZ.:
Rev. W. H. Hill,   Rev. E. J. Gosling,
Rev. J. F. Beddy,
Rev. Edward F. Arney (Vicar.)
VISITORS OF THE SCHOOL, VIZ.:
J. F. Brickdale, Esq. | Rev. J. Burden,
James Davies, Esq. | Rev. J. L. Dighton,
Edward Jones, Esq. | The Ven. Archdeacon
John Rolls, Esq. | Crawley.
The Deputation from the Worshipful Company of Haberdashers,
The Governors of Jones's Monmouth and Newland Charities,
The Company's Banner,
The Beadle of the Company, with staff,
John Curtis, Esq., (Clerk to the Company),
J. Ranson Curtis, Esq.
WARDENS OF THE COMPANY, VIZ.:
Wm. H. Mullens, Esq. | John Hunt Gosling, Esq.
Benjamin Edgington, Esq. | Drew Wood, Esq.
MASTER OF THE COMPANY,
William Butler Simpson, Esq.
Constables.

Order of procession at the laying of the chapel foundation stone, 1864

The changes brought about during Mr. Roberts's time as headmaster were profound and, in effect, transformed the place from a small struggling grammar school to a public school. This was done partly through the building programme and partly by changes in the statutes. Both depended on receiving the full interest on the investments of the charity. The first grants in this direction were in 1862 when £4800 was allotted to build a new schoolroom, chapel, vestry and two classrooms. Nothing happened for a time but criticism from Thomas Hare, the Inspector of Charities in 1862, and from Gladstone in 1863, led to action. Gladstone, as Chancellor of the Exchequer, had attacked the way charities were run, remarking that he knew of a charity in Monmouth, educating 100 boys, which had 320 acres in Deptford, 'and its income will, I am told, after no large number of years, be enormous'.[7]

A year later, the foundation stone was laid by the master in the presence of the mayor and corporation, five MPs, the militia band, clergy and choirs, the school, and the architect, William Snooke.[8] The buildings, 'designed in the Tudor style', were finished a year later and were opened with even greater ceremonial. The stone came from the Duke of Beaufort's quarries at Buckholt. The schoolroom was lit by pendant stars and warmed by Galsworthy Gurney stoves. The adjoining classrooms were small, 20ft by 15ft. The chapel was 62ft by 25ft, had a clock costing £100 by Moore of Clerkenwell, was lit by ten standard lights, each with twelve jets, the aisles were paved with encaustic tiles from Godwin of Lugwardine, and the reredos, in Bath stone, contained the Lord's Prayer, Creed and Decalogue in illuminated characters. The contractors were Collins and Cullis of Tewkesbury. During the building, the school operated in the wool warehouse at North Parade House.[9]

In 1865, the year the buildings were finished, one of the commissioners appointed by the Schools Inquiry Commission made a preliminary visit to Monmouth.[10] This was H.M. Bompas, a man more critical than Seeley, who was to influence the future progress of the school through his detailed reports on the way it was run. By this time John Endell Powles, a local solicitor, had produced a pamphlet arguing that William Jones did not 'found a seminary where the lower middle classes should virtually exclude the upper middle classes - but to promote education generally'. He advocated a larger school, better pay for the staff, modern science and languages, increased fees and boarders from all quarters.[11]

Mr. Bompas's report was on similar lines: 'The class of boys who attend the School are principally the sons of labourers and small tradesmen. The sons of professional men ... hardly ever attend, an objection being felt ... to their associating with the lower class of boys in the School. About half the boys ... are of a class who would normally attend National schools ... and many boys apply for admittance at the Grammar School in order to save the weekly payment and the price of books at the National schools'.[12]

He took a poor view of Mr. Snooke's new buildings: 'Unfortunately the architect has arranged the buildings in a most inconvenient manner and the ventilation is deficient ... the room in which the Classical boys are taught is too small for the purpose'. There had been two alternatives: to build facing the river, or to remove the whole school to a site above May Hill, but the place chosen was cheaper. He emphasised the problem caused by forbidding boarders, as 'boys from a distance lodge in the town without any supervision (producing) very bad effects on the moral character of some of them'.[13]

He deplored the system of electing boys to the school and this was something that bothered the town. A letter from 'An Old Grammar School Boy' in 1863 urged all Monmothians to attend the reading examinations held by the visitors for admittance to the school. He had just attended one and found that country boys were invariably preferred to town boys because only one of the examiners was from Monmouth. He appealed for 'more Town Gentry to be elected Visiting Examiners'.[14]

Mr. Bompas thought that, because of changes in education, the original plan of the founder could hardly be considered binding. He considered the post of lecturer should be abolished and a stipend of £50 given to one of the curates of the parish church to carry out his duties. He then gave four ways in which the school could develop. The mayor and corporation wanted a first class grammar school with masters taking boarders, capitation fees of £8 and £2, and 100 free places. The inhabitants wanted no boarders, but up to 400 free places with better salaries for staff. The governors advocated a bursar, a common hall and dormitories in the school as at Wellington. The lecturer, Mr. Watherston, wanted no boarders and high capitation fees. Mr. Bompas did not commit himself, but added, 'I may state in conclusion that the town of Monmouth, which is a quiet and beautifully situated county town, and will ere long be connected by different railways with all parts of England and Wales, appears to be particularly suited for a large school of any description'.[15]

In 1864 Mr. Roberts had completed a questionnaire sent out by the commissioners in which he had set out the number of boys taking each subject. Out of the 100 in the school, all took religious instruction, reading and geography; ninety-seven took writing and arithmetic; eighty-six history; seventy-six English grammar but only fourteen English literature and eleven composition; twenty-four Latin and eight Greek; twenty-six mathematics; twenty-four physics; nine book-keeping, and two drawing. No one took French, music, German or chemistry and the headmaster's chief problem was 'The bad English used by boys out of school'.[16] Compulsory chemistry had been introduced for all boys at Wellington in 1859, largely at the instigation of the Prince Consort.

The school prospectus, issued in 1870, giving a full list of the staff with their duties, illustrates the advances made in the first decade of Mr. Roberts's period as headmaster. Boys could apply for entry between the ages of 8 and 16 but could not stay beyond 18. The Classical School was open to any boys from England and Wales, the Commercial School to boys whose parents lived in Monmouth or the three neighbouring counties. Capitation fees were 30 shillings a quarter on the classical side and 10 shillings on the commercial. Any teacher could take boarders with permission of the visitors and boys could board in the town in premises licensed by them. Licensees had to keep to school times, provide separate beds, and were paid 7 shillings a week if they fed the boy, 2 shillings and sixpence if they did not. Books and stationery were paid for by the parents but there were three exhibitions of £50, two scholarships of £15 in the Classical School, and one of £10 in the Commercial.

The prospectus also contained twenty-five examination papers, showing the standard expected in Greek, Latin, divinity, French, German, geography, natural philosophy, trigonometry, mensuration, algebra, Euclid, arithmetic, history, English grammar and composition.[17]

Amongst the questions the headmaster was asked by the commissioners in 1864 was one concerning the occupations of the parents of the ten highest and ten lowest boys in the school. They were:

Parents of the ten highest	*Parents of the ten lowest*
auctioneer	shoe maker
butcher	farmer
boot maker	solicitor's clerk
clergyman	saddler
ironmonger	gentleman
schoolmaster	fisherman
spirit merchant	labourer
farmer	mason
schoolmaster	publican
butcher	timber merchant[18]

Only three of the ten highest came from Monmouth, whereas all but three of the lowest ones did. One other statistic which he provided concerned the age groups of all boys in the previous three years. They were:

Under 10   8 boys
Above 10 and under 14   63 boys
Above 14 and under 16   25 boys
Above 16   4 boys

With so few local boys staying at school after they were 16, and more than half being between 10 and 14, the examination papers in Appendix B are surprisingly difficult. Early leaving continued, and in 1919, when there were 101 boys from the town and county, only ten were over 15.[19]

It was hoped that the inclusion of specialists on the staff might induce the parents to leave their sons longer at the school. One such was Mr. Old, the dancing master. He was one of a musical family and amused K.M. Pitt by gliding amongst the dancers, playing the violin and shouting instructions at the same time. Once a year he gave a party at the White Swan and the dancing class put on white ties and white gloves and were allowed to dance with selected young ladies from one of the private academies. It was probably one of the first occasions in Monmouth when the opposite sexes were encouraged to meet by a member of staff.

A tradition of Christmas holiday concerts began in 1870. They were staged for the public by staff and boys, with the help of 'the Ladies of the Town'. They set a precedent for the establishment of music as one of the most effective ways of bringing the school and the town together.

The *Beacon* critic was appreciative: 'Altogether we have no hesitation in saying that this concert is one of the most enjoyable musical reunions of the year, and well deserves the distinguished patronage it obtains'.[20] A frequent visitor to both schools at the end of the century was Sir Walford Davies who could not understand why boys, perfectly capable of writing essays, were unwilling to try composing music, which was much simpler. Eighty years later the director of music could list eight composers from amongst the boys.[21]

Chapel services seem to have been choral throughout Mr. Roberts's time, the Sunday services being advertised beforehand in the local papers.

The organist and choirmaster in 1877 was M.T. Russe. He also taught piano, harmonium, singing and composition to private pupils. He lived in St. Mary Street,

PROGRAMME.—PART I.

Duet—Pianoforte and Harmonium—"Lurline," *Engel.*
Mr. H. J. Lewis and Mr. Holt.

Glee—"You stole my love." ... *Walter Macfarren.*
School Choir.

Song—"The Requital." ... ... *Blumenthal.*
Mr. Roseveare.

Solo Pianoforte—"The Lover and the Bird." *W. Kuhe.*
Miss Peppercorne.

Part Song—"O hush thee my babie."...*A. S. Sullivan.*
Miss Brookes, Miss Williams, Mr. Roseveare, and
Mr. Polgreen.

Song—"Night and Morning." ... ... *Cowen.*
Miss Williams.

Trio (Instrumental)—"Allegro Agitato." ... *Hummel.*
Miss Old, Mr. Old, and Capt. Bayliff.

Song—"The Grey Prior." ... . *T. Banks.*
Mr. E. S. Webber.

Glee—"Joy to the Victors." ... ... *A. S. Sullivan.*
School Choir.

Duet, Pianoforte—"Rigoletto." ... ... *Cunio.*
Miss Williams and Miss Peppercorne.

Song—"Beauty, Sleep." .. .. *Arditi.*
Miss Brookes.

Duet—"Convent Bells." ... ... *J. Blockley.*
Masters Bishop and Simmonds.

PART II.

Glee—"Sir Knight, Sir Knight, oh whither away ?'
School Choir. [*C. A. Macirone.*

Song—"The Boatswain's Leap." ... ... *H. Leslie.*
Mr. Polgreen.

Solo Pianoforte—"Concerto." ... ... *Mendelssohn.*
Miss Peppercorne.

Song—"Little Maid of Arcadee." ... *A. S. Sullivan*
Mr. B. S. Biram.

Part Song—"Daylight is fading." ... ... *H. Leslie.*

Song—"The Angel's Call" ... ... *Rita.*
Master R Courteen.

Solos Pianoforte—(*a*) Pasquinade ... ... *Gottschalk.*
(*b*) Rondo Capriccio *Mendelssohn.*
Mr. Holt.

Glee—"The Belfry Tower." ... ... *Hatton*
School Choir.

Song—"The Dream." ... ... *J. P. Knight.*
Master Chambers.

Trio (Instrumental)—"Allegro and Andante Grazioso,
Miss Old, Mr. Old, and Capt. Bayliff. [*Mozart*

Song and Chorus—"The Boys of Merry England."
Mr. Roseveare and School Choir. [*M. Hobson.*

Part Song—"Sleep gentle Lady." ... *Sir H. Bishop.'*
Miss Brookes, Miss Williams, Mr. Roseveare, and
Mr. Polgreen.

GOD SAVE THE QUEEN.

Concert programme, 1870

MONMOUTH GRAMMAR SCHOOL CHAPEL.
MATINS.

Preces and Responses ....*Tallis*
Venite ....*Lee*
Psalms .... *Woodward, Aldrich*
Te Deum ....*Barnby* in Bb
Benedictus .... *Crotch*
Hymns ....N.E. 368 ; N.E. 320, O.E. 207
Kyrie.... ....*Chipp*

EVENSONG.—6 30.

Psalms .... *Helmore, Reinagls*
Magnificat ....*Dyce*
Nunc Dimittis............... .. ..*Battishill*
Hymns ......N.E. 257, O.E. 317 : N.E. 232, O.E. 322
Hymn after Sermon.. ............N.E. 338, O.E. 364
Holy Communion at 12 noon on first Sunday in
each month.

Chapel services as advertised *c*1870

next door to a rival, H. Smith, who advertised all the same subjects, but with the added refinement that he would give his lessons in French, German or Latin.[22] A Nicholson organ had been installed in the chapel in 1886 and was opened in the following year by A.J. Eyre, the organist from the Crystal Palace. There are full technical details in *The Monmothian*, No. 4, 1886. Other activities were encouraged. There were amateur concerts in the schoolroom and plays continued to be performed on speech day.

By 1870 'Godliness and Good Learning', the ideal of Thomas Arnold, had given way to the 'muscular Christianity' foreshadowed in *Tom Brown's Schooldays*. But although compulsory games were becoming important, sports days still had a carnival flavour, with the militia band and the town cricket club's marquee from which the crowds watched running, jumping, throwing the cricket ball and dropkicking, the day culminating in an open race for a revolver. Cricket faltered, and there was a plaintive cry in the local paper that the school had a bat, a ball and stumps, but no field to play on.[23] The visitors agreed, suggesting that a field would be 'likely to prevent the Scholars associating with a lower class of boy during play hours'.[24] As a result a ground was rented from the Duke of Beaufort.

The rugby club which had begun in a haphazard way in the 1860s had a full fixture list by 1880 when, between November and December, they played Christ's College, Brecon (lost), Abergavenny ('Draw in favour of School by 2 touchdowns in defence'), Monmouth Town (drawn), Pontypool (lost), the Sixth Form (won), Newport (lost), and Chepstow (won).[25] The usual team line-up was two backs, one three-quarter back, two half-backs, two quarter backs and eight forwards.[26] Fifty years later it was two backs, two half-backs, two three-quarter backs and nine forwards.

In spite of an anxious letter to the *Beacon* in 1883, describing in detail the dangers of the scrum as a means of transmitting disease, rugby remained the most successful of the games played, and in 1886 R.P. Roseveare wrote to the *Monmothian* suggesting the setting up of an Old Monmothians' rugby club. He suggested that it could have as a nucleus C.H. Newman, captain of Wales; five other Welsh internationals, G.F. Harding, T.J. Clapp, T.B. Jones, J.A. Jones and C. Jordan; as well as several who had played for the universities. The idea was abandoned when only three old boys offered to play. But the school produced many fine players, especially in the years before World War I. In 1912 the Springboks came to the school and gave talks on the Bond of Empire.[27] A year later a school team beat Newport 1st XV, which contained nine internationals including T.H. Vile, by 14 points to 10.[28]

Rugby football as illustrated in the
Beacon, 1895

C. H. Newman,
Oxford University,
Newport and Wales, 1886

There had been rowing since 1858 when the crew wore white trousers, guernseys, and boaters bearing the name of William Jones in gilt. The school launched two new boats in 1889, one of them stroked by the headmaster. It bore a brass plate with the company's arms and 'William Groves, Master 1888'. He had been responsible for raising the money to pay for them.[29] Swimming had taken place near the mouth of the Monnow, but casualties led to many requests to the company for an enclosure in the river which might save lives until a bath was built. School blazers with wide black and narrow blue stripes were introduced in 1885, obtainable locally for 10 shillings and sixpence.

The new buildings opened in 1865 did not satisfy Mr. Roberts as, by 1870, there were 210 boys in the school and a waiting list of twenty-six.[30] He expounded his frustration before boys, parents and the company at speech day in 1870: 'I hope time is not far distant when the check to our progress arising from want of space, want of house accommodation, and want of appliances will be removed permanently, and that some provision for our immediate requirements will even be made before next half-year commences. It seems to me a great pity that at a time when nearly everyone is alive to the necessity of increasing the means of more thoroughly diffusing education through the country, a smaller number are being educated here than are willing to come and be taught'. There was a swift reaction from the secretary of the company who deplored Mr. Roberts's bad taste in criticising the Haberdashers before the assembled boys. Nevertheless the bad taste acquired three new classrooms by 1871, an enlarged chapel, library and laboratory in 1875, and the completion of the buildings in Wyebridge Street in 1878.

Through all these changes the opposition continued to oppose boarders, fees, and anyone entering the school from outside the borough boundaries. The leader was Mr. Cossens who managed to infiltrate a meeting in the Guildhall in 1871 by using a card which read 'Headmaster of Monmouth Grammar School'. Once inside he addressed the assembly before being asked to leave.[31] Mr. Roberts was furious when he heard about it, calling Mr. Cossens a liar and an impostor, but it was only a diversion because by 1870 Mr. Roberts had achieved his ambition of attending the Headmasters' Conference.

The extensions in 1878 met with Mr. Roberts's approval and he praised 'the handsome buildings going up, providing a spacious dining hall, commodious dormitories and excellent bath rooms'. At the same time Mr. Snooke, the architect, made plans for rebuilding the road between Wyebridge Street and Weirhead Street, and when the work was finished he entertained the seventy workmen employed by Collins of Tewkesbury to a substantial supper at the Queen's Head.[32] Unfortunately a large area of waste ground was left facing the river and this led to

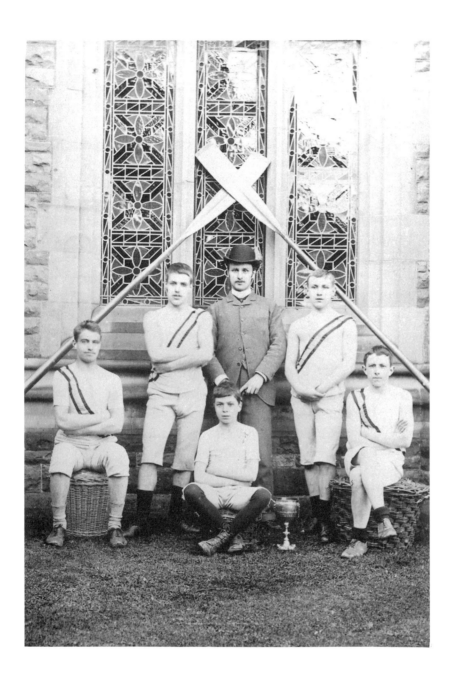

Winning crew, house fours, 1883, with Mr Roseveare

three increasingly angry deputations to the company, in 1881, 1882 and 1883, each complaining about the shabby state of that part of the school's property. The editor of the *Beacon* joined in with a ferocious editorial describing the disgraceful state of the ground and imploring the Haberdashers to accept the headmaster's suggestion that it should be covered by a swimming bath.[33]

In 1881 Mr. Roberts was interviewed by the Departmental Committee on Higher Education in Wales. He gave a detailed account of the school's progress, giving the numbers as 271, 'but the agricultural and commercial depression has affected us materially'. He was asked about his attitude to the worship of Nonconformists, and assured the committee that they were allowed to attend the chapel of their parents' choice, but had to give an account to a master as to where they had been. He went on to inform them that, in the school, there were 'Not twenty boys who were not Churchmen'. When asked how he knew this, he replied that on Ash Wednesday the whole school was given the choice of going to church or doing arithmetic, and only twenty boys did arithmetic.[34] It was not always arithmetic that they did. In 1889 a boy asked on Ash Wednesday to be allowed to go to the Catholic Church. Permission was given, but it was found that he had spent the whole time smoking a pipe in the schoolroom. He was immediately suspended.

In his speech at prizegiving in 1881, Mr. Roberts told the parents how important it was that the school should prepare boys to become craftsmen. To ensure this he had equipped a carpenter's shop for that purpose. The company had provided a lathe, and masters were encouraging their boarders to use the facilities whenever possible.[35] On the same occasion he made a surprising reference to the possibility of a girls' school being opened in Monmouth. He said that if the company could ever see their way to establishing such a high class school here, he was sure they would confer a boon on the town that could not be overestimated.[36] This was a complete turnabout from what he had told Thomas Arnold in 1875. He then stated, when asked his opinion, that such an institution would be deplorable, as 'it would lead to little romances in the streets, and boys would be distracted from their work'. It was not a problem that was going to concern him as he was to retire in 1891, a year before the High School for Girls was to open in what had once been one of his boarding houses, Hardwick House in Monnow Street.[37]

Mr. Roberts's last years were troubled ones, and undoubtedly the school was in decline and causing concern to the visitors. They wrote to the company 'conveying serious charges of inefficiency against the Staff' and sent a copy of their letter to the headmaster. He asked to be allowed to state his case [38] and the company agreed but wrote to the visitors assuring them that they would make any alteration to the conduct or personnel of the school that was necessary.[39] At the root of the problem

The Gramar School
Monmouth
12th Nov 1887

To the Master Wardens, and Court of Assistants
of the Worshipful Company of Haberdashers London.
Gentlemen;

It is with the greatest regret and surprise
that I received on Wednesday last a Copy of a
letter from the Visitors to your Worshipful Court,
conveying serious charges of inefficiency against
the Staff of this School.

I would therefore most respectfully ask you,
as Governors, to give us as Masters (most of us
of many years' service) the opportunity of repres-
-enting our views upon the subject, as we one
and all feel that we can give you ample
evidence on our side that the School has obtained
and still maintains the credit of faithfully and
well preparing the pupils entrusted to our Charge,
for the various Examinations and walks in life
which their Parents desire their Sons to enter upon.
I am, Gentlemen,
Your Obedient Servant
(Signed) C. Mc Roberts.

Letter from the headmaster to the company, 1887

was the examiner's report for 1887 in which he compared the Monmouth results with those at Friars' School, Bangor, where the boys had been asked identical questions. He divided the answers into four sections:

	Monmouth	Bangor
Excellent:	20	58
Good:	35	80
Fair:	57	128
Indifferent:	488	334[40]

The headmaster of Friars' School had no doubts as to why he had won ... boarders. 'Boarders', he wrote, 'are the very leaven of a School, they are the element which can most easily be manipulated'.[41] But as few people in Monmouth had heard of the Bangor school, the report was effective and led the visitors to accept the examiners' proposal of monthly examinations in which masters examined each other's classes, 'thus instilling wholesome rivalry amongst the staff'. Other suggestions included more oral teaching, carefully graduated classes, more practice and care in writing. In science and chemistry, boys should always write from memory a précis of preceding lessons. French and German were fair but would benefit if boys spent their holidays abroad.[42] These were matters for the staff; what worried the visitors was the number of dissatisfied parents removing their sons and sending them elsewhere.

One cause of discontent was the length of the holidays. An 'Inhabitant' wrote to the local paper asking what work had been done in the last fortnight. 'Masters and Boys have eight weeks holidays, and the probability is that upon Their return to School it will take a fortnight to get into working ? order, making a total of three months in comparative idleness ... It is a great shame that parents should have to pay for what they do not get'.[43]

The same troubles recurred in 1888 when delays over the introduction of a New Scheme under the Endowed Schools Act were causing distress to masters who were all getting too old to welcome further innovations. There was also concern as to whether the county was in England or Wales. This was important when Sunday opening, disestablishment and the Welsh Intermediate Education Bill were being debated. As early as 1885 the Conservative candidate for the borough had promised that he would vote for the exclusion of Monmouthshire from the Welsh Education Bill. But when the amendment was raised in Parliament it was quickly defeated and the bill received royal assent in August, 1889. It has been regarded as setting a precedent for separate Welsh legislation and as such 'one of the most impressive memorials of the political awakening of Wales'.[44]

But not everyone in Monmouth was pleased to be a part of this political awakening because it coincided with the local demand that more of the charity's money should be spent in Monmouth. As a result many parties attempted to forestall the New Scheme when the first draft came out. The school was to remain a grammar school for boarders and day boys; there was to be a new school for girls within the borough; there was to be an elementary school for boys and girls who had passed an examination in reading, writing and arithmetic and would pay sixpence and ninepence a week; and there was to be a Jones West Monmouthshire school which would admit boarders and day boys. It was this last proposal, to spend the charity's money outside the borough, which caused the trouble.[45]

The uncertainty which the delays over the New Scheme caused amongst the staff led all of them to offer their resignations in 1889. Between them they had completed 124 years of teaching, and had been the mainstay of the school for over thirty years. What troubled them was the clause giving the new headmaster power to dismiss any member of staff, who had then no right of appeal. Mr. Roberts, who had been headmaster for thirty-two years and was in poor health, asked for a pension but was instructed to stay on until the scheme came into effect. Mr. Earle, who had completed twenty-seven years and never sought promotion because he had been told that his post was permanent, was given a pension of £80 a year. Mr. Roseveare, who during his thirty-one years had bought a house for boarders which was too large for his family, was also pensioned. Mr. Pitt, who had taught for thirty-four years, was given a pension of £250 per annum, and the headmaster became rector of Brinkley in Cambridgeshire.

Meanwhile the effects of the New Scheme which emerged in 1891 troubled both the local people and the company. The scheme allotted annual grants of £2800 to the boys' school, £1000 to the new girls' school, £250 to the new elementary school, and £1000 to the West Monmouthshire school which was to be situated at Pontypool.[46] As if this dissipation of a local bequest was not enough, there was a further grant of £3000 to King Henry VIII Grammar School at Abergavenny, £6000 to found an agricultural school at Usk, while the residue was to go to the Monmouthshire County Council for unspecified educational purposes. Discontent was increased by almost all the estimates for the new buildings being greatly exceeded by the contractors.

As a result anger concentrated on the Charity Commissioners, and the governors sent a memorial to them in 1899 expressing their disappointment with the scheme. They pointed out that although a large library had been provided, 'it is entirely destitute of books, and further that the School is unprovided with a swimming bath, sanatorium, covered Five courts and carpenters' shop. They would also add that

The masters c1860: the Reverend C. M. Roberts (headmaster 1859-91),
William Pitt (second master, 1857-91), William Roseveare (1858-95), Robert Earle (1862-91)

a favourable opportunity now occurs of lighting the schools with electricity'. The local resentment against the commissioners had been expressed in 1885 in a frequently reprinted poem, *The Charity of Charity Commissioners.*[47]

By 1891 the opposition to change was running out of ideas, but a hard core of radicals kept returning to 1614 and William Jones. They were encouraged for a time by popular suspicion of the New Scheme, which had taken so long to come into force that few people knew what was involved.[48] This had affected the staff, and at his last speech day Mr. Roberts spoke of 'the three weary years of uncertainty' which they had undergone. In spite of this he was proud that in the thirty-two years he had been headmaster between sixty and seventy boys had gone to the university, whereas when he arrived in 1859 no one could tell him of anyone who had gone there. He then spoke enviously of the untold wealth available to his successor who would have £1000 more a year to spend than he had been given. It was a rather grudging speech as he and Mr. Pitt had been made to run the school for some months after they have been given illuminated addresses and superannuated.[49]

The new governing body (a fusion of the visitors and the company) had met before speech day and Mr. G.G. Griffin had become chairman. The final details of the scheme revealed the chief cause of Mr. Roberts's disgust: the salary of the next headmaster. He was to receive £200 and a capitation fee of £3 for up to 300 boys, with a guarantee that it would not be less than £600 in the first three years. He could also keep a boarding house with up to thirty boarders.[50]

Not unnaturally there had been ninety-one applications for this post, and the short list of six included masters from Uppingham, Westminster, Clifton, Dulwich and the Royal Institute, Liverpool. Their ages ranged from 28 to 36, and Hugh Culley aged 31, from Liverpool, was appointed. He was a double first from Balliol, with fourteen testimonials from, amongst others, the Bishop of Chester, Benjamin Jowett, T.F. Tout and Professor Ryle. In the following year, the failed applicant from Dulwich, F.W. Sanderson, became headmaster of Oundle and began his great reformation of the public school system.

Applicants for the headship filled in a complicated form which asked, amongst other things, for their special qualifications. The answers ranged from long essays on their previous life to one whose chief advantage was that his wife was a Welsh lady. One applicant began shyly, 'It is difficult to speak of one's own qualifications,' but then managed, 'I may say I have great powers of organisation, extraordinary fondness for the work, and power of maintaining absolute discipline without effort'. Many offered to bring boys with them, one almost his whole

The Charity of the Charity Commissioners

'Before I pass', the kind man said,
'To do some little good I'll try;
O Lord have pity on the poor!
And let me aid them ere I die'.

'Come Mr. Lawyer, draw a deed
And make it plain and make it sure;
I'll build a school and almshouses
That shall till time shall end endure.
The children shall be freely taught

That they may rise from low estate;
The old shall food and shelter have,
And find some comfort in their fate'.

'Write, Mr. Lawyer, for that end
I give this money and this land;
So word thy scroll that greedy heirs
May ne'er undo what I have planned.
See, here I set my hand and seal,
The poor shall have some blessings FREE!
And it may hap when I am gone
They'll sometimes kindly think of me'.

He died, and in succeeding years
The generations blessed his name;
And then some clever gentlemen
Down to this quiet township came;
Well-fed, fine-coated, pompous-voiced,
These high and mighty visitors;
'We've come to set all right', they said;
'We're Charity Commissioners!'

'What's this? A FREE school? Almshouses?
Bequeathed by Mr. So-and-so?
Tut! Tut! We'll all such nonsense end!
We what is best far better know!
The old fool must have doting been
About these common country curs;
We'll soon an alteration make.
We're Charity Commissioners!

The poor, indeed? Bequeathed for them?
Is there no workhouse or no gaol?
What! clothe and teach the young brats FREE?
And house the old? A likely tale!
We have a SCHEME to end such stuff;
Don't prate of 'rights' the will confers.
We'll our superior knowledge show!
We're Charity Commissioners!

Are there no sons of gentlemen
Who might reap benefits instead?
Some nice appointments might be made?
We have the power! We nothing dread!
The Poor? They're trampled every way;
And not a soul resentful stirs!
In this we'll do just as we like,
We're Charity Commissioners.

school. This was not unusual. Miss Luckes, when she moved from Hereford to start the Monmouth High School, brought some of her best girls with her, and when Henry Holden moved from Uppingham to Durham in 1853, he took a third of the boys with him, leaving his successor, Thring, with only twenty-five.[51]

Mr. Roberts's long reign had many positive aspects. The school began to emerge from its embattled shell and take an interest in the town. In 1869 the masters had planted hundreds of rose trees in the 'scandalously neglected cemetery'. The chapel had been enlarged and the company had provided a new Nicholson organ which was unveiled in 1866 by the organist from the Crystal Palace. Stained glass was placed in the chapel window, the central panel commemorating Mr. Roberts's son who had died when head boy.

In 1872, R.R. Webb became senior wrangler and first Smith's prizeman, and his success did much to change the usual critical attitude of the town to the school. He was presented by the mayor with a claret jug and waiter and speakers expressed delight that he had 'turned the hearts of his fellow townsmen'. The headmaster added his 'pleasure at so much good feeling on the part of the Town and neighbourhood'. The mayor asked for a holiday at 'the first fine day if we ever get one' and the meeting ended with cheers and a cold collation at the White Swan.[52] Four months later the inhabitants presented the school with a portrait of Webb so that 'the pupils ... as they look upon the portrait may be stimulated to strive to win the same distinction (which) has added a golden mark to the roll book of the School'.[53]

Boys began coming to school in trains, and in 1869 a boy appeared on a Velocipede. It had wooden spokes and rims and an iron tyre. K.S. Pitt, who was at the school at the time, then acquired an Acme penny-farthing which was no more of a success.[54] Seven Old Boys had gained international rugby caps, and had begun a tradition of fine fifteens, of which the 1955 team was probably the best, winning all eleven matches and scoring sixty-four tries with only three against.

School crews began to acquire boats from Oxford[55] and in 1880 an Old Boy, W.M. Warlow (junior), rowed for Cambridge. Cricket flourished, but not as widely as it should according to the editor of the *Beacon*, who thought that 'every boy should learn, as part of his education, to trundle the ball and wield the willow'.[56] Mr. Culley was to be called 'the second founder of Monmouth School', but in many ways Mr. Roberts had a better claim.

R. R. Webb

References

[1] *Monmothian*, Dec., 1936.

[2] MB. 1/8/1924.

[3] MB. 24/2/1864.

[4] SVB. 24/6/1854.

[5] SVB. 15/12/1862.

[6] SVB. 24/12/1864.

[7] A. Tilney Bassett, *Gladstone's Speeches*, 1916, 339.

[8] MB. 18/6/1864.

[9] MB. 29/7/1865.

[10] MB. 15/7/1865.

[11] *The Grammar School of William Jones*, 1864.

[12] Schools Inquiry Commission XX, 26. For the predominance of local boys see Admissions 1828-1868 in Appendix D.

[13] *Ibid*, 27.

[14] MB. 28/3/1863.

[15] Schools Inquiry Commission, XX, 30.

[16] See Appendix C where answers from Usk and Abergavenny are given.

[17] See Appendix B.

[18] Schools Inquiry Commission. Volumes for Monmouth are XX (1870) and III, *Answers to Questions*, 1868.

[19] SLB. 13/6/1919.

[20] MB. 5/12/1874.

[21] M. Eveleigh, *Hitting the Right Note*, 1922, 168.

[22] MB. 19/5/1877.

[23] MB. 4/12/1880.

[24] SVB. 24/9/1860.

[25] MB. 11/12/1880.

[26] MB. 3/3/1933.

[27] MB. 25/10/1912.

[28] MB. 28/2/1913.

[29] MB. 26/6/1858 and MB. 25/5/1889. See also Retrospect of the MGS Rowing Club in *Monmothian*, July 1882.

[30] For comparison: in 1868 Sedbergh had 13 boys and Giggleswick 37. (Schools Inquiry Commission, IX, 1868).

[31] MB. 6/5/1871.

[32] MB. 27/4/1878.

[33] MB. 6/1/1883.

[34] MB. 1/1/1881.

[35] Thring introduced a carpenter's shop at Uppingham in 1862 and Clifton was

given one in 1875.

[36] MB. 25/6/1881.

[37] Hardwick House held 35-40 boys, the food was excellent and in the 1880s there were four boys from the house in the Welsh XV. (T. Baker Jones, 1872-1879).

[38] See letter on p.77.

[39] SVB. 12/11/1887, 26/11/1887.

[40] SVB. 13/10/1887.

[41] E.V. Jones and J. Haworth, eds., *The Dominican*, 1951, 73.

[42] SVB. 3/10/1887.

[43] MB. 28/7/1887.

[44] K.O. Morgan, *Wales in British Politics, 1868-1922*, 102.

[45] MB. 27/7/1889, SVB. 19/7/1889.

[46] The cost of this school, designed by Henry Stock, was £23 340. (*The Builder*, 1898).

[47] MB. 14/11/1885.

[48] Approved by the Queen and published 23/2/1891.

[49] MB. 1/8/1891.

[50] MB. 13/6/1891.

[51] G.R. Parkin, *Life and Letters of Edward Thring*, I, 79.

[52] MB. 15/6/1872.

[53] MB. 12/10/1872.

[54] K.M. Pitt, *Monmouth School in the 1860s*.

[55] MB. 25/5/1889.

[56] MB. 20/7/1889.

6 HUGH CULLEY AND LIONEL JAMES: 1891 - 1928

The rosy prospect prepared for Mr. Culley in Mr. Roberts's last speech soon developed shadows. He had made sure before accepting the post that he had absolute freedom to choose his staff. As a result all the assistant masters were given a term's notice.[1] The only exception was Mr. Roseveare who was given the headmaster's house as Mr. Culley decided to have his.[2] He brought with him from Liverpool his classical master and the sudden dismissal of men who had served the school for many years led to much recrimination.

Mr. Peill, after twenty years in which he is credited with having introduced rugby to the school, was too old to find new employment and was reluctantly granted £50 to help him to emigrate.[3] M. Chollet, who had taught French for twenty-four years and was crippled with sciatica, was also allowed £50 so that he could return to Switzerland.[4] Others found new posts or retired to poverty.

Mr. Culley also miscalculated, as many have done, the willingness of Monmothians to welcome advice from newcomers. He had an unfortunate aptitude to rush into print with demands for a line of trees to be planted down the middle of Monnow Street, or that all the Monmouth music societies should amalgamate as there were too many inferior ones. This antagonised the antiquaries as well as the members of the inferior societies. He quickly made an enemy of the borough council by accusing it of immorality for only sweeping the streets for race meetings, 'when Monmouth teemed with a pestilential horde of bookmakers and their attendant scum ... lewd fellows with filthy manners and dirty language'.[5] A letter signed by 'A lewd fellow' replied that filthy manners and dirty language often occurred in the rugby matches which Mr. Culley was always encouraging his boys to take part in.[6]

A contemporary described him as 'very tall, very thin, walking with hands behind him, bent forward ... His whole appearance was fearsome and this impression was borne out by his severe discipline'.[7] But he mellowed, especially with the musically able. He was a good pianist and used to invite boys to supper and then play music with them afterwards.[8] Mrs. Culley, large and kind, wearing impressive hats, was well known in Monmouth, driving around in her dog-cart with a Dalmatian running beneath.

He was an able speaker, and at Headmasters' Conference in 1897 proposed that

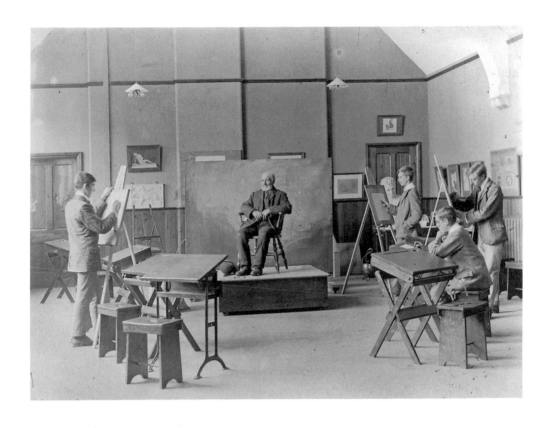

An art class *c*1900; the subject is one of the almspeople (*Monmouth Museum*)

'This Conference deplores the time wasted in teaching boys the present system of Weights and Measures and would welcome the adoption of a more rational system'. It was passed unanimously.[9]

Unfortunately, he tended to make speeches in school which were critical of his predecessor, and Mr. Roberts and his sons were quick to reply. The first objection occurred after speech day in 1901 when one of the sons wrote contesting the list of honours which Mr. Culley had claimed. He pointed out that four of the pupils were never taught by him, one was named twice, reducing the list to eighteen instead of twenty-three, and went on to recount his father's successes which, in the case of first class honours, outnumbered Mr. Culley's by ten to one.[10]

Mr. Culley began his reply, 'If the Reverend Harry Roberts was not an old pupil of mine, I should not notice his letter' - but he was and should have read what he criticised more carefully - 'How it brings back old times to me to find myself thus addressing my old pupil!' He had referred throughout to the school, not individual headmasters, and ended by recommending his old pupil 'to cultivate habits of clear thought and accurate observation'. This would make him 'a living testimonial to his old School'.[11]

As the former pupil was a naval chaplain on board HMS *Eclipse* in the China Sea, his father replied for him, accusing Mr. Culley of making no attempt to answer the letter, of throwing dust in the readers' eyes, and giving no examples of the alleged inaccuracies. He ended, 'when a misleading record is exposed, a flimsy pretence of explanation is worse than silence'.[12] Mr. Culley did not remain silent for long but confined later speech days to reports on basic facts such as 'putting the finishing touches to our sanitary system, which now represents the highest point to which the science of sanitation has advanced'. Enthusiasm in this field was caused by the new girls' school closing down a few days after opening at Hardwick House because of the insanitary conditions there.[13]

The news of this had spread as far as Liverpool and a letter has survived from a woman whose son had been taught by Mr. Culley in that city, asking whether it was safe to send him to Monmouth, as she had heard that the sanitary conditions there were so very poor.[14] She had reason to be afraid. In spite of it being a condition of entry that a boy had been vaccinated, epidemics of scarlet fever, diphtheria, measles and occasionally cholera continued to recur, while the main town sewer went on emptying into the Wye about one hundred yards upstream from the school well into the second half of the nineteenth century.

In 1900 the threat of increased fees rose again and a petition was sent to the

JONES' GRAMMAR SCHOOL.

Average Receipts and Expenditure for 3 years, ending 31st December, 1898.

RECEIPTS.

	1896.			1897.			1898.			Average.		
	£	s.	d.	£	s.	d.	£	s.	d.	£	s.	d.
Endowment	2,700	0	0	2,700	0	0	2,700	0	0	2,700	0	0
Repairs and Improvement Fund ...	100	0	0	100	0	0	100	0	0	100	0	0
Tuition Fees	702	13	4	721	13	4	718	13	4	714	6	8
Rent of Master's House, £50 0 0												
Less Tax ... 2 1 8———	47	18	4	47	18	4	47	18	4	47	18	4
Deficiency										302	19	7
										£3,865	4	7

EXPENDITURE.

	1896.			1897.			1898.			Average.		
	£	s.	d.	£	s.	d.	£	s.	d.	£	s.	d.
Masters' Salaries	2,294	0	0	2,302	0	0	2,311	0	0	2,302	6	8
Clerk's Salary	52	10	0	52	10	0	52	10	0	52	10	0
Printing and Advertising	77	12	10	39	18	0	68	9	4	62	0	0
Books, Stationery, and Prizes... ...	50	12	4	50	12	1	48	19	5	50	1	3
Coal and Wood	17	12	6	18	2	0	22	9	1	19	7	11
Gas and Water	57	15	7	62	3	9	54	12	4	58	3	11
Rates and Taxes	76	15	2	53	16	5	143	15	2	91	8	11
(The Poor Rate Assessment was increased in 1898 in consequence of the additions to the Head Master's House and new Class Rooms and Library, so that the rates in future will be considerably more than the average of the last 3 years. The reason why the rates of 1897 were lower than 1896 is that only one Poor Rate was collected in that year.)												
Scholarships	400	0	0	400	0	0	400	0	0	400	0	0
Exhibitions	480	0	0	480	0	0	480	0	0	480	0	0
Petty Cash Disbursements, including Porter's and Cleaner's Wages	72	9	9	81	14	2	83	6	8	79	3	6
Athletic Fund	15	0	0	10	0	0	10	0	0	11	13	4
Gymnasium	10	0	0	10	0	0	10	0	0	10	0	0
Examination Fees...	31	13	6	31	3	2	33	9	6	32	2	1
Rent of Field	24	3	4	24	3	4	24	3	4	24	3	4
Head Master's Petty Disbursements ...	21	7	10	15	17	1	11	17	2	16	7	4
Drill Instruction	15	4	0	14	12	0	14	12	0	14	16	0
Auditor	5	5	0	5	5	0	5	5	0	5	5	0
Fire Premium	9	4	0	8	17	5	14	12	6	10	18	0
Tradesmen's Bills...	104	8	11	17	5	7	12	17	6	44	17	4
Repairs and Improvement Fund ...	100	0	0	100	0	0	100	0	0	100	0	0
										£3,865	4	7

The school accounts, 1898

governors, signed by the mayor and 236 others, protesting against the idea: 'In our opinion the interests of this Borough will be seriously affected by such a course. The School has in the past been a great attraction by reason of its moderate fees and excellent education and we feel sure that if the fees are advanced it must diminish the number of scholars and entail loss to the Town'.[15]

Meanwhile the Monmouth Jones Charity Committee continued to hold boisterous meetings at which countless resolutions were passed, demanding more almshouses, greater pensions, an orphanage, houses for married couples, a technical college, apprenticeships, grants to emigrants, more scholarships and the usual hundred free places.[16] Letters continued to record the plight of the poor, one from the secretary of the Monmouth branch of the Independent Labour Party ending, 'Excuse my handwriting, spelling and grammar, as some other fellow has got my education which William Jones left for Me'.[17]

Editorials tried in vain to bring the opposition together, deploring the numerous minor objections, and warning that the Charity Commissioners could ignore them, especially as some were quite unreasonable. But the opponents of the commissioners had plenty of local support, and when Mr. Lawrence stood for the borough council as a representative of the Jones Charity Committee, he topped the poll and defeated a sitting councillor.[18]

In 1900 Mr. Culley's tongue again ran away with him. While birching a boy, the son of a local butcher, he called him 'a member of a worthless family'. The boy went home, reported the headmaster's words and revealed bloodstains. Mr. Culley was summoned before the local bench for using excessive force and fined £2 12s 2d. which included costs.[19] There followed an avalanche of letters to the papers marvelling at the folly of the magistrates and extolling the benefits of flogging. 'An Old Public Schoolboy' (Fettes) could never remember anyone not bleeding after a birching, while another from Abergavenny claimed to have been beaten every day of his school life, still had the marks on his body, and was happy to send his sons to the same place.[20] Some boys, indeed, did take pride in their ability to withstand flogging, but fear of it often led the more timid to avoid it by lying, and lying was usually more severely punished than other offences. On one occasion Arnold gave a boy eighteen strokes for lying and then found that the boy was innocent.

Arguments then returned to the wasteful characteristics of the Charity Commissioners where Monmouth was concerned. Luxurious palaces were being built for the boys and girls of wealthy parents while not a brick was being laid for the elementary school. The trouble here was that although the building, designed by

Henry Stock, the architect of the High School, had been completed in 1903, it was not opened until 1906. There was further discontent over 'the vast sums' spent on the grammar school masters who had fewer boys to teach. This was based on some disputed figures which showed that in 1886, when there were 207 boys in the school, the staff salaries came to £1799, whereas in 1900, with only 160 boys, the salaries came to £2336.[21] 'A Lover of Justice' countered this argument by stating that there were many teachers who, after thirteen years service, were earning less than two pounds a week.[22]

One of Mr. Culley's best letters was in answer to yet another 'Native of Monmouth' who wanted to know whether Overmonnow children were getting a fair share of the school. He assured the writer that, provided the child could bring the three Cs, Character, Capacity and Conduct, and pass a simple examination, he would be welcome whatever his social background. 'But', he wrote, 'it is quite another thing to propose as a native of Monmouth proposes, to make the Grammar School a sort of Chapel of Ease, with a bonus of £10 a head for St. Thomas's School (Overmonnow) ... In four years we have had only three candidates, one of them got only two marks for his Arithmetic and the others did but little better'. Elementary schools were free for such children, the county council provided scholarships for them to advance to a grammar school, and every native of Monmouth should be grateful to the tax payers who had made this possible.[23]

Mr. Culley resigned from ill health in 1906.[24] During his time at the school the number of buildings had greatly increased, his aim having been to provide accommodation for three hundred boys. He did not achieve this, but the syllabus was widened and included a class of thirty doing optical shorthand in 1898. A cadet force was formed and began exercising in uniform in 1905 when they carried out an attack on Redbrook. W.M. Warlow published his *History of the Charities of William Jones at Monmouth and Newland* in 1898, and for the first time a well researched history of the school from its foundation was available for 7/6d. Marcus Holmes, a pupil of Herkomer, was appointed art master, and speech days were enlivened by boys acting scenes from Shakespeare, Aristophanes and Molière.

These were positive achievements when so much of his time was involved in complicated discussions with commissioners, governors, local education authorities, the borough council, the editor of the *Monmouthshire Beacon*, and the William Jones Charity Committee. Above all he was faced, for the first time with the presence, on the other side of the town, of the High School for Girls, and all the social complications this involved.

The OTC, 1909

He was followed by a man of similar belligerence, Lionel James, who had been sixth form master at Radley. His election was difficult as, after the post had been advertised, the LEA objected to the salary offered and threatened to withdraw its grant. In consequence those on the short list were asked if they were willing to accept a reduced capitation fee. Some refused. There was further trouble over a memorandum signed by many Old Boys asking that Mr. Roseveare should be appointed. When he was not, his brother, the Reverend R.P. Roseveare, wrote asking why. The clerk had to reply very diplomatically.[25]

So Lionel James arrived to face opposition from the Old Boys, disquiet from the staff who foresaw their own salaries being reduced, and a broadside of advice from those inhabitants still hankering after the celebrated hundred free boys. He was usually a match for them, but soon fell foul of the Board of Education which was becoming increasingly bureaucratic, demanding endless returns, time tables, expense accounts and registers. He infuriated that body by referring all their demands to the school clerk who had to invent the answers.

Mr. Culley had received no pension and Lionel James pacified his staff by beginning a campaign for a proper pension scheme.[26] It took nearly four years, but by 1900 it was ready. He then concentrated on completing some of Mr. Culley's buildings, and in 1908 the new art block, lecture hall and laboratory were complete.

Lord Tredegar, a veteran of the Charge of the Light Brigade and honorary colonel of the Royal Monmouthshire Royal Engineers, was asked to open them. The buildings had been designed by R. Page FRIBA and built with local stone from Mr. Griffin's quarry by J.H. Leadbetter of Newport. On the appointed day, Haberdashers, civic dignitaries, governors, the cadet force and important visitors assembled around the red carpet at May Hill Station. Unfortunately Lord Tredegar alighted at the other side of the town on the deserted platform of Troy Station. There were a few minutes when the cadet force prepared to double down to Troy, while Lord Tredegar was being bundled back into his carriage. But this delightful prospect was wrecked by Lady Llangattock speeding through Monmouth in her car to collect him and bring him back to the red carpet at May Hill. His opening remarks dwelt pointedly on the need for proper organisation, something from which he had already suffered in the Crimea.[27]

The people of Monmouth could now compare the examiners' reports on the two Haberdasher schools, and for a time the advantage lay with the High School, described in 1909 as 'One of the happiest and brightest schools which the inspectors have visited ... The School is not merely a pleasant school, there is health and strength in the whole of its life'.[28] In 1909 both schools were placed on the list

Lionel James (front, centre) and staff, *c*1909

The Grammar-School Monmouth

Monmouth Grammar School

FOUNDED BY WILLIAM JONES

A.D. 1614

Head Master

L. JAMES, Esq., M.A., late Westminster Scholar of Christ Church, Oxford.
1st Class Honours, Classical Moderations; 2nd Class, Literæ Humaniores.

Assistant Masters

A. W. WISEMAN, Esq., M.A., Mus. Bac., late Scholar of Gonville and Caius College, Cambridge, 18th Wrangler. Senior Mathematical Master.

J. L. ENTWISTLE, Esq., M.A., London, Hon. B.A. Manchester Victoria University; Associate and late Prizeman of the Owens College, Manchester. *Second Master and Master of the Old House.*

A. S. LITTLEWOOD, Esq., M.A., late Scholar of University College, Oxford; 1st Class Honours, Classical Moderations, 2nd Class, Literæ Humaniores.

J. E. BRIGGS, Esq., M.A., late Scholar of Clare College, Cambridge, 2nd Class Honours, Natural Science Tripos.

R. H. WILLIAMS, Esq., B.A., late Scholar of St. David's College. *Master of Town Boys.*

R. CAMOUS, Esq., B.-ès-Lettres, Paris, University of Heidelberg, (Modern Languages.)

Rev. W. O. JONES, University of London, Senior Master of the Mercantile Department.

R. W. M. DUNDAS, Esq., B.A., Keble College, Oxford.

N. C. ELSTON, Esq., B.A., Keble College, Oxford.

DRAWING—MARCUS HOLMES, Esq., late Herkomer Scholar, Associate of Bristol Academy of Arts. *Master of Country Boys.*

ORGANIST AND CHOIR MASTER—C. H. PAYNE, Esq.   DRILL AND CADET CORPS—Lieut. R. W. M. DUNDAS

GYMNASTICS—The Instructor in the Monmouth Gymnasium (Corporal BLAKE, late 1st Batt. Essex Regiment.)

JOHN BELLOWS, GLOUCESTER 25607

The school prospectus of 1906

of secondary schools authorised for grant[29] and were already advertising in the GWR handbook, *Holiday Haunts*, half a page to each school.

Mr. James, used to the peace of the Radley countryside, then renewed the demand for his school to be rebuilt on the other side of the river, away from damp, dirt and constant disturbance from 'street cries, noisy children, motor-cars, steam-rollers and barrel-organs'. Only there could it face on equal terms the new building dominating the town from the Hereford Road.

There was little chance of such a wholesale move taking place, though Lionel James continued to use its desirability as an excuse for getting improvements on the existing site. But by 1910 he had settled down and, with the help of the governors, had established rules which were to control the future development of the school. They were approved by the Board of Education and set out in widely dispersed leaflets.[30]

They continued to differentiate between the classical side, with tuition fees of £10 a year, and the mercantile side at £6 a year. These fees covered all subjects in the curriculum and the use of equipment and paper. They did not include printed books or mathematical instruments. These were paid for by parents and belonged to the boys. Boarding fees were to be not more than £50 a year and were additional to the tuition fees.

Charges for optional subjects were paid in advance each term and were: gymnastics at the town gymnasium in Glendower Street - 3s. 4d; cadet corps - 7s; pianoforte lessons - £1 16s 8d; organ lessons - £2; shorthand - 10s; special drawing for engineers and architects - £1 1s; outdoor sketching - £1 10s; athletic sports - 3s 4d. There was also a day boys' preparation class which cost 5s a term.

There were twenty exemptions from tuition fees, called Monmouth Scholarships, for boys from the borough of Monmouth, ten of them for preference for boys who had spent not less than two years in a public elementary school. There were ten exemptions for the administrative county of Monmouth and ten foundation scholarships open to unrestricted competition. Lionel James had advertised the latter, which were worth £20, in six papers in 1906, including the *Spectator* and the *Birmingham Post*, and got only two replies. This was to be expected, he said, as adjoining schools were advertising scholarships of £80. The number of exemptions for boys from Herefordshire and Gloucestershire was to be determined by the governors in consultation with the LEA All boys whose fees were exempted were to be called scholars, although another document referred to them as bursars.

A memorandum in 1910 showed where the boys came from:

	Classical Side	Mercantile	Total
Abroad	7	1	8
Breconshire	1	0	1
Carmarthen	2	0	2
Cheshire	3	0	3
Glamorgan	8	3	11
Gloucestershire	17	5	22
Herefordshire	13	9	22
Ireland	1	0	1
Lancashire	5	0	5
London	1	0	1
Monmouthshire	33	58	91
Northamptonshire	2	0	2
Staffordshire	2	0	2
	95	76	171[31]

An 1888 memorandum was less detailed:

	Classical	Mercantile	Total
In the Borough	17	60	76
In 10 miles	9	30	39
Over 10 miles	72	30	102
	98	120	217[32]

The Welsh Department of the Board of Education's inspectors, Owen Edwards, W. Edwards and B.B. Skirrow, carried out an inspection in 1909 and commented on the fact that it was part grammar school and part secondary. In spite of this they thought it 'especially suited for pupils who are to enter the Universities and the liberal professions. The tone of the School is excellent and appears to be in a thoroughly efficient condition'. Their opinion of the buildings was not so high. They approved the new science and art wing, but the older rooms were too near the street, depressing in outlook, furnished with long desks which should be replaced by modern tables. Corridors were inconvenient and too narrow. There was no cloakroom, inadequate lavatories, no suitable dining room for day boys, no school gymnasium, poor ventilation and lighting, and no pictures. More and better classrooms were needed as well as a better carpenter's shop. The excellent staff and exceptionally good attendance deserved better surroundings.[33] It is almost as

The science laboratory, *c*1905

The carpenters' shop, *c*1905

if Lionel James had written it himself, as he had already angrily voiced all these problems to the governors in the year after he arrived.

In fact, he disagreed with almost every word of it and presented the governors with a well-printed copy, with 'some remarks of the Headmaster' on the opposite pages. He denounced the report on five grounds: The omission of fundamental problems such as 'the starved revenue of the School'; erroneous theories on the scope and nature of the school; suggestions that were mutually destructive; failure to draw logical conclusions from their own premises; and errors and omissions of fact. He compared it unfavourably with the inspection of 1904 which had reported that a school of 140 boys required eleven assistant masters. In 1910 he had 168 boys and only nine masters, all 'scandalously underpaid'. He was infuriated with the comment on pictures when he had spent £20 out of his own pocket to provide them. He contested the proposal that the classical and mercantile sides should be combined, on the grounds that the boys from private schools came at the age of eight or nine and stayed for up to eight years, while boys from elementary schools came at twelve and rarely stayed for more than two.

In the section on buildings, the inspectors had criticised the distance between the lavatories and the assistant master's boarding house, and were told that the boys got chilblains tramping across the yard at night. They suggested an underground lavatory. Mr. James thought this would have a deplorable effect on 'both health and morals. The more fresh air in this department the better for both body and mind'. The inspectors had ignored the lack of fire escapes, bathrooms, drying rooms, studies and the fact that the organ gallery in the chapel backed on to the sick room. Above all he was appalled that they had made no attempt to uncover the financial restraints under which he had to operate.[34]

So in 1912 he and Mr. Entwistle proposed a scale of increased salaries which was approved by the governors. What they became is shown in the first column. The adjoining column shows the salaries at the High School for Girls for comparison:

J.L. Entwistle	£300	Miss H.M. Jackson	£90
A.W. Wiseman	£200	Miss I.F. Twigg	£85
A.S. Littlewood	£250	Miss S.E. Fish	£80
J.E. Briggs	£220	Miss W.G. Brown	£75
R.H. Williams	£200	Miss W.E. Schmidt	£60
Rev. O. Jones	£190	Miss M.P.N. Harty	£60
R. Camous	£220	Fr. M. Kuster	£60
M. Holmes	£136	Miss. M.E. Shepherd	£60
N.C. Elstob	£140	Miss Nott	£50

C.H. Pearson	£120	Miss Lodge	£30
F.P. Wood	£100	Miss C. Rickards	£80
Miss Cossens	£37 16s 0d	Miss E. Payne	£80
M. J.A. Chollet	£50	Mr. M. Holmes	£30
		Miss Metcalfe	£59 18s 6d
		Pianist (Dancing)	£4 10s 0d
		Miss Guest (Secretary) £15	

Lionel James as headmaster had a fixed salary of £200 and a maximum capitation grant of £500. Miss Carless as headmistress of the girls' school had a salary of £100 and a capitation grant on 134 pupils of £89 6s 8d a term. Neither was allowed to incur any extraordinary expenditure above £2 without getting the permission of the clerk to the governors. It was expected that the senior masters would remain at the school until they were 60 and that the junior masters would probably leave in under five years.

The headmaster then attacked the alienation of the endowment to the county council. Under the 1909/10 scheme there was an annual grant of £2800 to the Grammar School, £1000 to the High School, and a similar sum to West Monmouthshire School. The residual income of the charity went to the county council which, in return, gave grants totalling £1300 to the three schools. It was not until 1955 that this was rectified when West Monmouthshire School was transferred to the county council, and most of the residuary income returned to Monmouth. By then the Education Act of 1944 had offered to fee-paying schools a direct grant of £29 per boy in return for 25 per cent of the annual entry of free places. In this way Monmouth School became a direct grant school.

Having failed in this, but improved the salaries of his staff, Lionel James turned his sights on the conditions in which his masters were compelled to teach. His target here was Mr. Page, the Haberdashers' architect, who had designed a new boarding house for thirty boys. The headmaster insisted that such a house would not pay its way and that the building must be capable of taking forty boys.[35]

The sum available was £4850 and Mr. James proposed three possible sites, Wyeside, Ivy Bank (The Royal George), and Wyesham. Unfortunately all the estimates exceeded the money available, Wyeside by £500, Ivy Bank by £350 and Wyesham by £1850. But the site at Wyesham had already been promised £700 and Lionel James was willing, if the governors authorised a public appeal, to guarantee any deficit. This made the Wyesham plan the cheapest.

But the governors were wary of having their hands tied by a donation from the

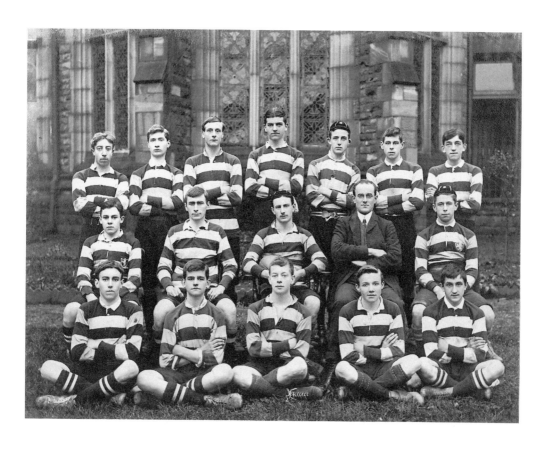

School 1st XV, 1913 (Angus Buchanan front row, left)

headmaster, however small, and at a meeting from which he was excluded, they voted to place the new house on part of the school playground. This was exactly what he did not want and he subjected all sides to an avalanche of objections. He argued that such a site would add to the congestion, deprive him and the housemaster of a garden, place the house too near the river mists, cause antagonism by rejecting a gift of £1000, and above all deprive the school of a wonderfully healthy position at Wyesham. The only objection to that site had been the distance from the school. He had paced it. It was 630 paces, so 'any active boy can be at the School in 3 minutes and on the playing fields in one'. It was of no avail, a new boarding house arose from the playground and was opened in 1914.

As war became inevitable, precautions began to be taken. The OTC changed from blue uniforms to khaki (Monmouth is reputed to have been the last school to wear blue). Parts of the playing fields were dug up to plant potatoes; and many of the younger boys found that their fathers were preparing to go overseas. It was not to be long before some of the older boys joined them.

'Wholesale War', screamed the headlines of the *Beacon* on 31 July 1914, but at first Monmouth took little notice. In the following week the regimental sports took place on Vauxhall, the reredos in the school chapel was redecorated in mosaics and speech day took place as normal. The orchestra, founded in 1912, played the Toy Symphony by Romberg, boys acted scenes from *A Midsummer Night's Dream*, and the headmaster launched an impassioned appeal for money with which to celebrate the three hundredth anniversary of the foundation of the school.[36]

He listed seven absolute necessities, costing not much more than £2000: the enlargement of the playing fields, improvement of the pavilion, restoration of the fives courts, improvement of the schoolroom, provision of an organ for it, decoration of the chapel's bare walls, and the acquisition of certain properties near the boarding house. The main appeal would be for between £5000 and £10,000 for a scholarship fund. He hoped to have the money by the end of the year. He then returned to his favourite theme, the penury with which the company surrounded him. Eight years ago, when he had appointed school monitors, he had promised them that their names would be recorded on boards for posterity. He was glad to announce that he had at last acquired the trifling sum which would allow him to keep his promise.

Several members of the staff were called up. M. Camous joined the French army and was invalided out in 1916, Mr. Elstob became a captain in the Monmouthshire Regiment, (his brother Lt-Col. W. Elstob gained an MC, DSO and posthumous VC), F.P. Wood was commissioned into the Border Regiment, and two others

The Frogs of Aristophanes, 1909

(*left to right*) F. Whitfield, H. Daintree, S. Edwards, R. Scott, E. May,
E. Edwards, D. Lawton, D. Mackintosh
(*foreground*) H. Watkins

joined up later.[37] The governors decided that if an exhibitioner joined the forces before he completed his course, the money would be held over so that he could complete it on his return.[38]

Thereafter James became one of the leaders in the town's war effort. The cadets embarked on night marches, trench digging and signalling exercises.[39] D.G. Hogarth, the keeper of the Ashmolean Museum, addressed both schools on the causes of the war; matches were played to raise money for the troops; concerts and dances were organised for them; the school's rifles and playing fields were offered to those men between thirty-eight and fifty-eight who formed the National Training Volunteer Corps. In exchange the OTC was given Italian rifles, one foot longer than their Lee Enfields, and almost impossible to drill with[40] and from the end of September the *Beacon* published a weekly Roll of Honour, recording the names of the many Old Boys serving in the forces.

On the civilian front James was equally active, ensuring that sports days, concerts, and prizegiving continued as usual. He helped to found the Monmouth Improvement Association which held its first meeting at the school. Because of transport difficulties, he organised a daily motor service for girls and boys coming from the Forest of Dean.[41] He arranged for it to be used by adults if there was room, but does not seem to have made clear that fares had to be paid, and long after the war, the school clerks were writing to parents for payment for journeys made by their sons many years earlier.

W.M. Warlow died in 1918. His grandson had died of wounds in 1915. In that year sixteen Old Monmothians were killed; a year in which, during the first two hours of the Battle of Loos, more British soldiers died than in all three services on all sides on D-day, 1944. And as the casualties mounted, so did the decorations, culminating in Lionel James's welcome in November 1917 to the blind Angus Buchanan. He had been head of the school and gained a £40 exhibition in 1913. When war broke out he enlisted and took part in the Gallipoli landings. He was wounded at Suvla Bay, but returned to the Peninsula and won the military cross at Helles. He then transferred to the South Wales Borderers and won the Victoria Cross in Mesopotamia. During an attack an officer was lying in the open severely wounded, about 150 yards from cover. Two men went to his assistance and one was hit at once. Captain Buchanan went out and carried the wounded man back under heavy machine gun fire and then returned to bring the other man. He went back to the front in 1917 and was hit in the head by a Turkish sniper, losing the sight of both eyes. He was mentioned in despatches four times and received the Russian Order of Saint Vladimir. He returned to take up his exhibition and, in spite of total blindness, became a successful solicitor. In some ways he embodied both the

Angus Buchanan VC by the school war memorial

horror and the heroism of that war, and very suitably he unveiled the school memorial to the seventy-six Old Monmothians who died. In his speech he hoped that the simple granite cross, designed by T.R. Bridson, would 'never be a mere ornament, but always a true and lasting monument to those who gave their lives'.[42]

Lionel James's grandiose plans to celebrate the tercentenary of the foundation of the school had been forgotten during the war and in 1920 he regretfully agreed that it should 'stand over'.[43] But the need for money was even more desperate, and as if to emphasize the school's poverty, he wrote to the *Beacon* in 1921 stating that he had seen in Simmonds' Olde Curiosity Shoppe, a painting of the old schoolroom by J.A. Evans which he thought the School should buy. Mr. Simmonds had agreed to keep it on show until the £7 needed to buy it had been raised. The headmaster asked for donations towards the cost. Three months later the money had been raised, and in thanking the donors, he hoped that he would be able to find the £2 necessary for framing it within the school.[44] The auditor was also becoming anxious about the finances and in 1919 had refused to sanction school funds being used on meals for the governors when they attended meetings. They reluctantly agreed to pay three shillings each time they had a meal there.[45] The company had been more generous in earlier years, offering £10 for refreshments in 1846, but it had been 'respectfully and decidedly declined'.[46]

The speech day in 1919 was important because the prizes were presented by the Reverend H.P. Prosser, the first Old Boy to become master of the Haberdashers. He was the grandson of the lecturer Prosser who had combined that office with being vicar of Monmouth in the 1820s. Lionel James, stating there were 283 boys in the school, claimed that it was imperative to provide accommodation for 400. Thus more money was needed, and that meant raising the fees to acquire more staff. Increased numbers and a heat wave had made it a difficult term. But his new system in which marks were abolished and replaced by competitions between forms, which were judged by the number of 'votes' and 'black marks' the boys had gained, had been so successful that detention had been abolished. In his speech Mr. Prosser approved of the system which he claimed to have suggested twelve years earlier. He seemed to be the only one there who understood it.[47] The inspectors in 1922 had been equally impressed: 'The spirit of healthy rivalry ... in the novel competition of class-work between Forms grows into a fine *esprit d'école* which shows itself in the playing fields and the after careers of the boys'.

Esprit d'école had been very evident on the river in 1921, when in a race between the school and Hereford Cathedral School, both boats had been swamped by a sudden wave as they passed Dixton church. Lionel James saw it happen and dived in to rescue the Monmouth cox, but the head of the school, G.H. Sutherland, was

Monmouth School by J. A. Evans, painted *c*1920

drowned trying to help other members of the crew. He was to be commemorated by the sundial in the school close and by Cruttwell's Island. This fatal accident, the second to a boy while Lionel James was headmaster, seems to have affected him deeply.[48]

In the year that Angus Buchanan won his VC, one of the school's most brilliant all-rounders was killed. H.W. Thomas left the school with an exhibition for King's College, Cambridge. He graduated with honours, having made a name for himself as actor and musician. He was also a fine outside half, playing for Wales against South Africa and England. During the match against the Springboks in 1913, in the dying minutes, when the scores were equal, he had dropped a goal which everyone at Cardiff thought went over. The referee disagreed. When his death was announced in the local papers four years later, there seemed to be more concern over the referee's decision than over the death of a young man doing what was expected of every junior officer, leading men to death in the face of massed machine guns and uncut barbed wire.

The appalling cost in lives during the war united the two schools and, more important, brought the town and the schools together. The 1920s consolidated this by the part the staff began to play in local affairs. The Reverend Owen Jones, who for many years had run the Monmouth Sports Club, was elected to the town council in 1920 but was not allowed to speak as he was a clerk in holy orders. He had to stand down, but was eventually elected.[49] Captain Elstob had no problems in getting on the council and eventually became mayor and chairman of the bench. Lionel James, who had been a founder of the Amenity Association and the League of Nations Union, was a lay reader, and on the board of the governing body of the Church in Wales. By constant letters to the *Beacon* he kept the council on its toes.

He had also to face the growing importance of women as MPs, mayors, magistrates and committee members. There was still a fairly rigid ban on communication between the two schools, but K.C.R. Howells, who had sisters at the High School and was a day boy at Monmouth, acted as courier, collecting letters before he went home, giving them to his sisters to deliver and returning the answers to his colleagues on the following day. In later life he realised how foolish he had been to make no charge for the service. There does not seem to have been any attempt to enlighten the boys about sex until Mr. Cullingford began lecturing on the subject after World War II. Nevertheless Lionel James supported the suffragist move-ment, and allowed the first political meeting solely for women to be held in his study.

His reaction to what the *Beacon* always called 'The Red Danger' was more complicated. He founded a school parliament at which on one occasion Clifford Tucker bravely moved that 'during the heroic struggle of the South Wales miners no blackleg or imported coal should be used in School grates or boilers'. The motion was lost by 144 votes to six.[50] More serious was a letter from 'A Parent' to the *Beacon* in 1924, asking on whose authority a party of grammar school boys was brought to Agincourt Square to cheer socialist and communists who had congregated there to spread their poisonous propaganda.[51] In a dignified reply Lionel James said that parents should have the courage to sign their names and write to the headmaster. He had allowed senior boys to watch Ramsay Macdonald's car pass through Monmouth during the general election of 1924.[52]

But in 1928 the *Beacon* published an appreciation of A.E. Williams on his retirement. He had been in charge of mathematics, rugby and swimming. The article said he would be keenly missed.[53] A week later Williams wrote thanking the editor but adding, 'I am not retiring. I have been dismissed by the Governors on account of my religious and political views'.[54] The letter he had received from the clerk to the governors had been bleak: 'I am directed by the Governors to terminate your engagement ... at the end of next term'. He asked why and was told that they had given no reason, nor were they obliged to. Backed by the Assistant Masters' Association, he asked for an interview. Letters between the clerk and the governors agreed that he knew perfectly well their reason and went on to describe him as 'a square peg in a round hole, in many ways quite out of sympathy with the aims and traditions of the School'.[55]

He had acted as agent for a Labour candidate at the 1924 election and wrote to the *Beacon* apologising for the failure of a speaker to turn up at a meeting in Raglan. Although it took two years, this letter seems to have started the campaign to get rid of him. He was ahead of his time as at the 1929 election two Old Monmothians entered Parliament - the Reverend Gordon Lang (Labour) for Oldham and Frank Owen (Liberal) for Hereford.

James had allowed one of his masters, Robert Cruttwell, to take over an island on the Wye and plant it with shrubs and flower beds in memory of G.H. Sutherland. It later acquired a band-stand, two weather shelters and seats for sixty-five people.[56] Not everyone thought it improved the view downstream from the bridge and some wrote to say so. Band concerts were held there, a girl was accused of stealing one of the flowers, the bridge leading to it was said to be dangerous, and vandalism and flooding led to its closure after the great flood of 1929. His other gift to the school had been the Bricknell Library, founded in memory of an Old Monmothian killed on the Somme.

Cruttwell's Island, *c*1925 *(Monmouth Museum)*

Cruttwell also become involved in correspondence with the local Baptist minister over an application he made for a licence to provide intoxicating drinks at a Town House supper in the Rolls Hall. Mr. Tucker, the minister, thought it 'unworthy and entirely unnecessary', especially as an extension had been asked for. Mr. Cruttwell replied angrily that there was no law forbidding children to enter licensed premises and that intoxicants would not be accessible for the boys. The editor closed the correspondence before Mr. Tucker could reply.[57]

In a long letter to *The Times* in 1926, James had written of the frustration of many schools on being deprived of staff and money by the provisions of the 1891 scheme.[58] He felt sure that schools such as Bedford and St. Paul's were affected in the same way as Monmouth. But in 1927 Town House was opened. He called it 'the realisation of a dream', town boys at last coming into their own on equal terms with country boys and boarders. It had taken him twelve years but had been worth it. It symbolised the uniting of town and school. Argument over the mythical hundred free boys could be forgotten while the school, the company and the town united to defeat the conspirators in the Board of Education who were depriving them of the money their founder had left them.[59]

James may have been an admirable teacher of the classics but he was beset by mathematical problems brought on by the introduction of the Burnham Scale and the Teachers' Superannuation Act. The Departmental Committee on Teachers' Salaries had stated in 1919 that the assistant teachers at the school were receiving only 56 per cent of what was their due.[60] The governors seem to have been aware of this as they had already complained to the Board of Education on the 'harmful effects of competition ... which have a tendency to induce teachers to transfer their services to the highest bidder'.[61]

In spite of this the governors were in no position to sanction any increase in salaries, as in 1920 the clerk informed them that their bank balance was 'almost zero'.[62] James reckoned that the introduction of the Burnham Scale would cost the school £927 in the first year, £1368 in the second, and £1605 in the third.[63] The deficits continued to increase until 1927 when the clerk complained, 'We are living very much from hand to mouth'. By 1928 he reported an overdraft of £1193 17s 6d, and in 1929 one of £2177 17s 6d.[64] This was in spite of raising the fees in 1922 from £12 to £25.

The increase had caused an uproar at the time, Captain Elstob on the town council having to face a furious onslaught from Councillor Jones who claimed to be the last free boy alive, his father not even having to pay for his slate and pencils.[65] By now there was confusion over what was meant by a free boy, a letter from the clerk to

MONMOUTH GRAMMAR SCHOOL

NAME, &c.	Age		Length of Service		Present Salary exclusive of War Bonus	Salary applicable under the Local Education Authority's Scale	REMARKS
	Yrs.	Mos.	Yrs.	Mos.			
Lionel James (Head Master), M.A., Oxon.	51	4	13	4	£700		House free of Rent, Rates and Taxes in addition.
Johnson L. Entwistle, M.A., Lond., Hon. B.A., Manchester University ..	57		28	2	£400*	£400 max.	
A. Sidney Littlewood, M.A., Oxon. ..	52	9	27	10	£350*†	£400 max.	
Rhys H. Williams, B.A., Lampeter ..	53	7	25	6	£290*†	£400 max.	Receives £20 in addition for Special Duties
The Rev. W. Owen Jones	49	3	22	10	£240*	£400 max.	
James E. Briggs, M.A., Camb.	51	10	21	10	£290*	£400 max.	
R. Camous, B-ès-Lettres, Paris	46	4	16	2	£290*	£390	
Marcus Holmes (part time teacher) ..	45	7	13	10	£160*		Receives £45 per annum in addition for Special Duties
Noel C. Elstob, B.A., Oxon.	35	5	12	2	£220*	£330	
Cyril H. Pearson, M.A., Oxon.	33	4	10	10	£220*	£300	
Wm. R. Irving, B.A., Camb.	27		5	2	£150*	£250	Receives £15 per annum in addition for Special Duties
Philip H. Heap, B.A., Manchester ..	25		4	2	£250*†	£240	
John F. R. Daniel, M.A., Oxon. ..	37		1	6	£250*	£360	11 years' previous service
(Miss) Kate Elizabeth Rafter	27	6	4	7	£120*	£200	
Arthur E. Williams, B.Sc., Univ. of Wales	32	9		2	£300	£300-£315	10 years' previous service

* Teachers marked thus receive £20 War Bonus in addition.

† These three Masters are Teachers of the Advanced Course in Classics whose salaries, as they stand at present, have been increased from the Advanced Course Grant. One defect of the County Scale is that it makes no provision for additional remuneration for posts of special responsibility, or for Honour Degrees. For this and other reasons the Governors would prefer to adopt the Scale of Salaries laid down in the report of the Departmental Committee of 31st July, 1918, on Teachers' Salaries, rather than that of the Local Education Authority.

Staff salaries, *c*1920

the governors in 1928 claiming that out of 145 Monmouthshire boys in the school, thirty-three were paid for by parents, twenty-three by the county council, nine by the scholarship fund, one by the Welsh Children fund and seventy-nine were free.[66]

James was now ill, and after an unfortunate incident in which he beat a boy, expelled him, and then took him to court, he resigned. He was remembered by many as an inspiring teacher of the classics, and at Radley had produced acting translations of plays by Plautus, Terence and Aristophanes. On arrival in Monmouth he wrote a school prayer book, *Jubilate Deo*, which went to a third edition in 1940. He also wrote *Songs of Zion*, an anthology for the plain man, consisting of psalms, 'freed from the bondage of the verse paragraph'.

In retirement he wrote a life of William Sewell, the founder of Radley, under the title *A Forgotten Genius*. Sewell was involved in the Oxford Movement and James equated him with Arnold as one of the founders of the public school tradition. He had many ideas for the reform of that system; the admission of one free boy in every ten; that the school should be a family; and that love not fear should be the bond of school life and discipline. But Sewell admitted that he 'never liked boys as boys' and was a strong advocate of the educational importance of pain, using both cane and birch fairly frequently.[67]

James agreed with most of this and quotes approvingly a conversation in which Sewell jokingly described a flogging room, 'a chamber removed out of hearing where at midnight the criminal boy may be brought from his bed to his master, masked in black; and then at each stroke, a toll of the great bell might announce the fact to the rest of the trembling dormitory'. There is no evidence that Sewell went to such lengths but he describes a curious scene after flogging two boys, 'When they got up from their knees they came to me and burst into tears, and put their arms around my neck and kissed me - as a child would his father'.[68]

Those who were at Monmouth in 1912/13 recalled the great flogging scene when all were summoned to Big School by Lionel James. 'The three delinquents, of whom the chief was to be expelled afterwards, were lined up near the door, the School Porter at hand to prevent them bolting. Then James came slowly forward on the platform, flapping his gown like a huge black bird, working himself with words into fury, his knuckles white on the reading desk. He flung off his gown and went into action ... the late Angus Buchanan, VC had the task of holding them down'.[69]

Did the educational value of pain have some effect on the heroism of those who died a year or two later in the mud and slaughter of Flanders? Looking back through speech days in the first decade of the century one gets an inkling of the words behind the acceptance of death in such appalling conditions by so many in that war: the emphasis on death in battle in classical times, on manliness, loyalty, athleticism, obedience and school songs which so affected Churchill and Rosebery (who asked for the Eton Boating Song to be played at his death-bed). Edward Thring summed it up in a letter: 'The learning to be responsible and independent, to bear pain, to drop rank and wealth and luxury, is a priceless boon ... with all their faults ... the public schools are the cause of this manliness'.[70]

The alternative to flogging, or its accompaniment, was expulsion, and the reasons for this ultimate disgrace show a strange variety, ranging from absence without leave, enticing other boys into pubs, talking to a girl for more than two minutes, and in the case of the chapel organist, playing *Yes we have no bananas* as a voluntary. The last-named was eventually reprieved.[71]

James with two other Old Monmothians, founded the Orbilian Society to publish a termly Latin newspaper, *Acta Diurna*. It was very successful and had a wide circulation. The name of the society was taken from Orbilius, a schoolmaster described by Horace as 'plagosus', fond of flogging.

An innovation which was not to James's liking was the introduction of the wireless. It came to his notice that a boy had been caught trying to do his homework while wearing the headphones of his crystal set, struggling with algebra while listening to a dance band. Could parents allowing such behaviour sink any lower?[72]

An Old Monmothian remembered that James 'always wore a thick dark grey tweed suit (he once extolled the virtues of good thick Welsh flannel to a boy he was about to cane), or else a snuff-coloured knickerbocker cycling suit with many straps and pockets ... We knelt at the breakfast table while he said prayers, and then while we ate our porridge he would disappear at a brisk walk to return a few minutes later, even more briskly. He had been for his morning run across the bridge'.[73]

References

[1] SLB. 31/7/1891.
[2] SLB. 6/8/1891.
[3] SLB. 8/4/1893.
[4] SLB. 18/9/1903, 25/2/1904.
[5] MB. 10/3/1899.
[6] MB. 7/4/1899.

[7] R.R. Farmer (1897-1902).
[8] L.E.L. Dowding (1898-1906).
[9] MB. 1/1/1897.
[10] MB. 9/8/1901.
[11] MB. 16/8/1901.
[12] MB. 23/8/1901.
[13] MB. 27/2/1892.
[14] VA, VII. 6. pkt.III.
[15] Copy in VA.
[16] MB. 24/4/1896, 22/10/1897.
[17] MB. 10/12/1897.
[18] MB. 5/11/1897.
[19] MB. 15/6/1900.
[20] MB. 2/6/1900, 29/6/1900.
[21] MB. 14/12/1900.
[22] MB. 21/12/1900.
[23] MB. 23/2/1895.
[24] MB. 1/6/1906.
[25] SLB. 1905, 118, 120, 125, 138, 160, 204.
[26] SLB. 1905, 309.
[27] MB. 24/12/1909.
[28] MB. 16/10/1908.
[29] SLB. 8/6/1909.
[30] SLB. 28/5/1910.
[31] SLB. 1909-1911, 188.
[32] SVB. 11/10/1889.
[33] VA. 1909.
[34] *Ibid*.
[35] Original correspondence in VA.
[36] MB. 7/8/1914.
[37] SLB. 4/12/1916.
[38] SLB. 30/11/1915.
[39] MB. 9/10/1914.
[40] MB. 5/3/1915.
[41] MB. 16/11/1917.
[42] MB. 7/10/1921.
[43] SLB. 9/11/1920.
[44] MB. 11/3/1921.
[45] SLB. 13/3/1919.
[46] SVB. 15/12/1846.
[47] MB. 5/8/1921.

[48] MB. 18/3/1921.

[49] For his chequered career on and off the council, see *Early Days of the Monmouth Labour Party* by Clifford Tucker.

[50] MB. 27/2/1920.

[51] MB. 24/10/1924.

[52] MB. 31/10/1924.

[53] MB. 2/3/1928.

[54] MB. 9/3/1928.

[55] SLB. 527, 534, 555-561, and C. Tucker, 'A Monmouth Boyhood' in *Gwent Local History*, 1977, 35.

[56] MB. 12/6/1925.

[57] MB. 18/12/1925, 15/12/1925.

[58] MB. 22/10/1926.

[59] MB. 29/4/1927.

[60] SLB. 21/10/1919.

[61] SLB. 27/1/1920.

[62] SLB. 15/10/1920.

[63] SLB. 15/2/1921.

[64] SLB. 25/5/1928.

[65] MB. 6/1/1922.

[66] SLB. 18/1/1928.

[67] *A Forgotten Genius*, (Faber, 1945).

[68] A.K. Boyd, *History of Radley College*, (Oxford, 1948), 98.

[69] W.A. Thorpe (1912-1920) Extracts in *Monmothian* 1935 and SVB. 16/12/1836.

[70] G.H. Parkin, *Life and Letters of Edward Thring*, II, 196.

[71] School Detention Book, 1873/4, *Monmothian* 1935 and SVB 16/12/1836.

[72] MB. 4/3/1932.

[73] *Monmothian*, Jan. 1962.

The school before the A40 bypass was built

7 RECONCILIATION: 1928 - 1995

After an interval of a term, Lionel James was succeeded by Christopher Fairfax Scott. He had been educated at Lancing, went to Oriel in 1913, joined the Rifle Brigade in 1914 and was invalided out in 1915. He returned to Oriel and then became an instructor in the Japanese navy. In 1919 he moved to Siberia to study Russian and eventually joined the staff at Cheltenham College. Then after barely seven years' teaching in the United Kingdom he became Monmouth's new headmaster. He tended to be a bird of passage, leaving in 1936 and proceeding to Brighton College and Hereford Cathedral School before taking a less onerous post at Truro Cathedral School.

But on arrival he lost no time in presenting the governors with a list of improvements needed. He divided them into Urgent (central heating £8000 and improvements to the headmaster's house £2000); Less Urgent (further improvements to headmaster's house £1500, gymnasium and manual training room £4200); and Desirable (swimming bath £2500, tar paving playground £600).[1] He was to be successful with a gymnasium in 1934 and a swimming bath in 1935.

During the 1920s the lecturer took on the name of warden and Monmouth Grammar School became Monmouth School. This last change caused some comment, especially amongst Old Monmothians, and at their dinner in 1929 certain differences appeared between Horace Bailey, proposing the health of the school, and the headmaster. Mr. Bailey thought that it should be the aim of the school to 'fit boys for the ordinary associations of life, rather than to specialise in producing a few geniuses'. After all, the average person had only average ability, yet the average man was the backbone of the nation.

Mr. Scott, in reply, agreed that 'the average chap made the country what it was'. He was in favour of 'the good sound chap, but in order to get him they must produce first class fellows with brains and fellows who are athletes'. Only then would they find parents from all over the country trying to get their boys into the school, which should contain at least 500 boarders. 'Unless we do this we will have to scrounge for every little blighter we can get'.[2] According to H.A. Ward, Scott was adept at touring prep schools and 'scrounging little blighters'. Once he had captured them he made sure that they behaved like gentlemen by attending regular cap-raising parades on the tennis courts.

He advertised the school extensively, sending leaflets describing the boarding bursaries and scholarships far and wide. This was in spite of the fact that there had always been some visitors and governors who thought that advertising the school was degrading. One of the charges against Miss Luckes, when she was dismissed from the High School in 1907, was that she was advertising 'cheap education in the *Spectator*'.

But Scott was sure that advertising was necessary and he soon came into conflict with the Board of Education over numbers. In 1934 he reported that the average number of boys to a master was nineteen. Masters had three free periods a week, and the sixth form worked unsupervised for six periods a week. He then became trapped in a bureaucratic maze involving school fees, the Burnham Scale, parents, governors, and the number of boys.[3]

His old headmaster from Cheltenham came to the rescue at speech day in 1929, returning to the purpose of all such schools still teaching the classics. He thought they should ask themselves what their pupils would be like at the age of forty. His answer was, 'intelligent reflective people with hobbies and interests of their own'.[4] The subject was pursued by the Provost of Oriel in 1931 and by Field Marshal Sir William Robertson in 1932. The former congratulated the boys on being taught in one of the most beautiful valleys in the kingdom[5] and the latter for having the most westerly OTC in Britain.[6] Both emphasised at length the virtues of hard work. Unfortunately for the headmaster, Lionel James continued to pour advice into the pages of the *Beacon* from his home in Sussex. Some did not affect the school, such as his instructions to the council on how to drain and build their new housing estate at Wyesham, but others did.[7] He became involved in arguments about the way to honour William Jones. A statue had been proposed in Agincourt Square; he preferred Wye Bridge. But he then suggested that a copy of the founder's will should be printed and placed in every Monmouthshire school, in the county education office in Newport, and at the Board of Education in Whitehall. If this could be arranged he would pay for printing the copies in especially large type.

He was supported by Sir Joseph Bradney, but the subject became side-tracked because James had said that William Jones was not a Welshman. Bradney had said he was, and James replied that it did not matter as the money was left to Monmouth. He then attacked the education department as 'blind stewards', strangling the growth of the school instead of helping it to become 'a large public school on English lines'.[8] Bradney replied in Latin verse that as James was a Cornishman he belonged to Wales and should not forget it. As a result the will did not appear all over the county, though I am told there was a copy in the window of a house in St. Mary Street at about this time.

In spite of trouble over finance, the numbers grew to 248, central heating was installed throughout the school, the chapel organ was adapted to electricity, and as well as the gymnasium and swimming bath, a new wing was added to School House. And as a special honour, Prince Arthur of Connaught became the first member of the royal family to visit the school.

But the admission fees continued to trouble both the town and the counties. The matter was raised by Councillor Breakwell, an Old Monmothian, at a meeting of the Monmouthshire Education Committee in 1934. He thought it scandalous that men, not earning enough to pay income tax, but wanting their children to be taught at the school, should have to pay £15 if living in Monmouth and £25 if in one of the neighbouring counties. When he was at the school, the admission fee was £2.[9]

Just before Christmas in 1936, Nicholas Penn Young, a boarder, climbed out of his dormitory window and went to May Hill Station where he stood in front of a train and was killed. The inquest revealed that he had written a letter to a girl and given it to a day boy to deliver. It was found by a master who read it and spoke to Young. It was an offence which Young knew was punishable by expulsion, though the master who found the letter maintained that he did not threaten the boy in any way. The coroner had no hesitation in finding a verdict of suicide whilst of unsound mind. There were others at the time who questioned the evidence. The fact remains that the letter was quite innocent, 'such as deceased might have written to his sister', and the boy was only sixteen. His grave at Dixton is marked by a small wooden calvary.[10]

Scott moved on to become headmaster of Brighton and Captain Elstob took over until a new headmaster was appointed. This was to be W.R. Lewin of Bruton and Trinity, a master at Blundell's. He was to face many problems when war broke out, some personal and some national. The first of these was to prepare for the evacuation to Monmouth of children from Birmingham.

The governors had been told that this would happen and had replied that it was impossible. But on 1 September 1939, 350 boys and thirty masters and helpers from King Edward's School, Five Ways, Birmingham, arrived at May Hill Station. The Monmouth reception committee was under the impression that a girls' school was arriving, and had lined the roads with Girl Guides to welcome them, but as soon as the Guide leaders realised what was getting out of the train, they quickly marched their charges down to the Rolls Hall where they were given the even more enjoyable task of escorting the boys to their billets. As so often in an emergency, it was left to Captain Elstob to sort the matter out.

The outbreak of war three days later unsettled the headmaster who made several attempts to join the Home Guard, and then the Royal Armoured Corps. He was unsuccessful and resigned in 1943 after being mistaken for a ghost against which the boys went to their dormitories armed with cricket stumps. His influence on the school was limited by his war aims but he had strong views on reform. In 1937 he had stated that 'a school must be remade in each generation or it will become dead. Many reforms will be made, but Old Monmothians will never see the new generation practising the Nazi or Fascist salute'. In his short time at the school, the war made reforms very difficult, but he launched an appeal for a new pavilion, and persuaded the governors to provide a free place to a young Jewish refugee from Germany.[11]

At speech day in 1939 he made a strong attack on the school certificate examination. 'The very last thing we want this School to become is a School Certificate factory. School Certificates have little to do with education. They are an unmitigated nuisance. We are very thankful when our boys are able to dispose of the nuisance easily and early. But they must then resume their education. If your boy has sufficient ability to get his certificate while he is still young, do not punish him ... by stopping his education at this point; give him his chance of sixth form work. If he is going to the University, he must have it. If he is not, then the sixth form represents his last chance, in all probability, of getting a real education'.

His was a voice crying in the wilderness. On speech day after speech day examination statistics continued to play an important role. Throughout the war the school was run by Captain Elstob and he certainly did not decry their importance, especially as for much of the time, comparisons could be made with Felsted, evacuated to Goodrich, and King Edward's, evacuated from Birmingham to Monmouth. Felsted looked after itself, but King Edward's had to share Monmouth's school buildings. This meant Monmouth using them in the morning and Birmingham in the afternoon. In spite of the complications this caused, not more than one and a half hour's teaching was lost in the week. It was one of the most successful of all school evacuations as the headmaster of King Edward's believed strongly in the value of country life in a town boy's education and did everything he could to develop it.

So all available buildings were used as hostels: smallholdings with pigs, chickens, goats, geese and rabbits were set up; large quantities of potatoes and peas were grown; and when the drift back to Birmingham began, the headmaster encouraged as many as possible to remain. The last boys returned in July 1944, when the parents presented the town with a plaque expressing their gratitude for the welcome they had received and the bonds which had been forged by such a very successful and co-operative visit.[12]

Four hundred and twenty Old Boys served in the forces during World War II and sixty-one of them gave their lives.

One of the results of the war was a joint speech day with the girls' school in the Rolls Hall.[13] It was probably the shortest ever recorded, lasting barely three-quarters of an hour. The idea was soon abandoned, but according to successive accounts of these events, it is surprising how rarely any of those presenting the prizes managed to say something original. Lord Raglan in 1942 was perhaps an exception when he said that the object of education was to turn boys into civilised men, successful men and good citizens. He defined the civilised man as 'one who took an intense interest in things of no use to himself or anyone else'. He thought the successful man one who found himself at fifty where he wanted to be when he was twenty, and the good citizen as one who subordinated himself to the interests of the community where he lived. The trouble was that the three objectives did not necessarily mix; a successful man was not always civilised, a civilised man was rarely a success, and good citizens often became the slaves of the successful. It was for the school to provide the mixture which would produce the best men.[14]

At his last speech day in 1946, Captain Elstob could report that the numbers had risen to 375 and should before long reach 400. He continued to help with mathematics and then became a governor. When he died in 1963 he had served the charity in different roles for fifty-six years, and was proud of the fact that he had never missed a single day from ill-health. He was remembered by many for the power of his voice which, when he was teaching, could be heard far down Almshouse Street, and for his many services to the community, as magistrate, mayor and church warden. He is commemorated by the choir stalls in Dixton church, and by the gates bearing his initials, NCE, on the river path through the churchyard.

He was followed as headmaster by Cecil Cullingford who came from Oundle, confessing that it was a sobering thought that Sanderson, the great educationalist and the second founder of Oundle, was not good enough for Monmouth in 1891 when Hugh Culley had been preferred. It made him very sensible of the problems which confronted him now that the endowment on which the school originally depended was also being used for three other schools.

In his first year he had maintained that one way of judging a school was by the number of Old Boys who sent their sons there, and announced that he hoped 'to turn out boys who know how to use their leisure and are not lost when they are out of reach of a cinema or a radio set'. For much of his time Mr. Cullingford was involved with the Butler education act of 1944 and its effects on the finances of the school. But it was not until 1955 that the West Monmouthshire School was transferred to the county council and the majority of the income from the charity returned to the town for which it was intended. The two Monmouth schools thus became independent fee-paying schools and quickly launched an appeal for bursaries to support children whose parents could not afford the full fees. It took the company some time to accept this decision as its finances had been affected by the destruction of the hall in an incendiary raid in 1940. It was not to be reopened until 1956.

Mr. Cullingford had a distinguished war record, serving with the 1st Battalion The Welsh Guards, then as chaplain to the 1st Battalion The Grenadier Guards and senior chaplain to the 79th Division in the invasion of Europe. His experience there made him eager to help others who fought. In spite of some opposition, he appointed Otto Maciag, who had served with the 1st Polish Armoured Division, to teach art, and other Poles, Mr. Hardulak to take music, and Mr. Materklas as school boatman. But he combined his many kindnesses with a tendency to let his words outrun his judgement, and like many of his predecessors he had trouble with the townspeople, on this occasion over school uniform. During the war local tailors had been unable to supply the required clothes and a London firm had taken their place. In 1950 the Monmouth Chamber of Commerce complained that Mr. Cullingford had entered into a new contract with the firm. They passed a resolution disagreeing with his action and disapproving of parents having to buy their boys' clothes from the school shop rather than from the shops where some of them worked. The headmaster remained adamant, maintaining that local traders had lost the contract by default during the war. But it was soon found that Burtons in Hereford could supply identical uniform at half the price.[15]

Contact between the school and the High School for Girls remained limited. G.C. Thomas (1940 - 1947) remembered as head of the school that any boy caught talking to a girl for more than two minutes would be punished. Each school tried to confine its pupils to certain roads for Sunday walks. Thus no boy was allowed to use the Hereford Road and girls were to avoid St. Mary Street. Relaxation of these rules came slowly.

During World War II there had been occasional joint play readings in the headmaster's study, and a combined choral society was formed. Some boys had been invited to a dance at the High School in 1942 to celebrate the engagement of C.W. Trow to a mistress there. Mr. Cullingford did not approve and it was not until ten years later that the roles were reversed and sixth form girls were asked to a

LOCAL TRADERS PROTEST

Monmouth School Headmaster's Action

LONDON FIRM TO SUPPLY SUITS

Parents Compelled To Purchase Through School Shop

The Headmaster of Monmouth School's decision to contract with a London firm for the supply of school suits has led to a strong protest being lodged by the Monmouth and District Chamber of Commerce.

At a special meeting of the Chamber held on Tuesday evening, a resolution was unanimously passed disagreeing with his action and strongly disapproving of parents being compelled to buy their son's suits from the school shop to the complete elimination of local traders, who had not been given an opportunity of tendering for the suits at competitive prices.

A copy of the resolution is to be forwarded to the Headmaster (the Rev. C. H. D. Cullingford) and to the Governors of Monmouth School.

Protest from the Chamber of Commerce

dance at the school. Segregation on the trains remained a problem, as it had been since 1907 when monitors from both schools had been appointed to see that there was no mixing in the carriages. The closure of the railway by Dr. Beeching eventually solved that problem. But there was little change until 1965, when the head boy invited the four heads of house at the girls' school to discuss ways of making 'rapprochement' between the two sixth forms. Mr. Cullingford seems to have had doubts as to how far rapprochement was meant to go, but decided to give talks on sex which he accompanied by film-strips. Over at the High School they employed a peripatetic teacher to give an annual talk on this hazardous subject.

Mr. Cullingford tried to encourage contact and co-operation between schools within the town. He was very aware of the social gap between 'schoolmasters' and 'teachers', and attempted to bridge it by inviting teachers from all schools in Monmouth, infant, primary and secondary modern, to tea with his staff in the common room. In the same period there was an attempt to co-ordinate the syllabuses of the top forms in the primary school and the first forms at Monmouth School in such subjects as maths, English and history.

He was equally eager to encourage a real partnership with the parents, impressing upon them on many occasions that the chief aim of the school was to instil the right use of leisure and the importance of leadership through discipline. Over the years he elaborated these aims to include the production of Christian gentlemen, the harmonization of science and the humanities, 'and a type of education which was noble and generous and gave an enduring vision of greatness'.[16]

He was to become increasingly critical of the growing influence of theorists, educational, political and administrative, who from their comfortable offices were ordaining how teachers should teach.[17] This was a theme that was to be taken up by one of his successors, Robert Glover. Cecil Cullingford deplored the introduction of GCE, an examination altogether inferior to the old school and higher certificate. Mr. Glover was to fight interference with the direct grant system on many of the same grounds.[18]

Mr. Cullingford, a keen caver, and the author of two authoritative books on the subject, encouraged boys to accompany him on expeditions underground in many parts of the country. He believed in all types of adventure training, outward bound courses, continental holidays, geographical camps. But he was well aware of the importance of the arts. He was a competent pianist and through the Royal Academy of Music enlisted Michael Eveleigh to the staff in 1950. The success of that move can be deduced from Michael Eveleigh's review of music at the school between 1946 and 1986 in 'Hitting the Right Note'.[19] The visual arts, in the hands

127

of Otto Maciag, flourished and the school received welcome publicity when in 1973 he made plaques of Wojtek the Bear for the Imperial War Museum, the Ottawa War Museum and Edinburgh Zoo. The famous bear had accompanied the Polish forces throughout the war and symbolised their courage and fortitude.

Although the Haberdashers' architects have rarely enhanced the Monmouth landscape with a masterpiece, the company has saved many of the town's finest houses from neglect and ruin. The process started when Mr. Cullingford acquired the Malt House in St. Mary Street in 1954 and converted it to Tudor House. Other headmasters followed in his footsteps, acquiring St. James's House, The Grange, Chapel House, Ivy Bank (temporarily), and more recently, Glendower Street Board School as a music centre and the Gloucestershire House as a maths centre. Within the school, Cecil Cullingford quickly converted the School House kitchens and introduced central catering. In the days when boys had their meals where they boarded, the food had varied widely. In 1900 H.M. Long remembered term after term of porridge and treacle for breakfast and bread and butter for tea and supper, whereas Mr. Pitt's house was renowned for good living: hot joints, stew or cold meat every day for dinner; sweet and soup once a week for supper, and a glass of beer for all boys over twelve at dinner daily.

One of Mr. Cullingford's most important objectives was the erection of the Shrine of Remembrance to the Old Boys who had died in World War II. It occupied the old choir vestry behind the chapel and was dedicated by the Archbishop of Wales in 1950.[20] Throughout his time at the school Mr. Cullingford pursued, in his own words, 'the hard right rather than the easier wrong'.

He was uncompromising in this and sealed it in his last disagreement in 1955. This involved a meeting with the governors about the new buildings which he believed were too near the swimming bath. To convince them he took along a highly amplified and orchestrated tape-recording of the noise coming from the baths which he had made that morning. It was unsuccessful and he was given the option of resignation or dismissal. Reluctantly he wrote, 'As I have been unable to agree that the Development Plan submitted to the Governors for altering and rebuilding this School deals adequately with its varied needs, and it is right that when these alterations take place the Headmaster should be in full agreement that they are the right ones, I am obliged to submit my resignation to the Governors, and I shall leave the School in a year's time, next July'. His hope that they would not accept the resignation was unfulfilled.

His experience with the Welsh Guards was carried over into the school and common room. He was intolerant of inefficiency and was meticulous in his choice of new staff. He offended the occasional parent, but maintained that his time at the school covered the golden years of his life. He died in 1990 asking that his ashes should return to Monmouth as an indication of his abiding affection.[21]

He was followed in 1956 by J.R.M. Senior who had been in charge of history at Shrewsbury and then headmaster of Bury Grammar School. His stay was short but he did much to encourage links between school and town, becoming chairman of the committee which ran a succession of Monmouth festivals. These introduced professional musicians and actors into Monmouth as well as lecturers like Sir John Betjeman and Hugh Trevor-Roper. After the ending of the festivals, the Merlin Music Society emerged which more than anything else was to open the school to the town and vice versa.[22]

Mr. Senior resigned for the same reasons as Mr. Cullingford: 'constitutional difficulties and disagreements with the building plan adopted for the School'. A few weeks later the Oxford and Cambridge representative on the governing body also resigned and the school lost its seat at the Headmasters' Conference. Senior's trouble had been the destruction of six teaching spaces before new buildings had replaced them, which meant forms being taught in inadequate accommodation like the fire station, Big School and the RAF hut.

But such rapid changes worried the parents and letters appeared asking why plans, seemingly causing so much trouble, were kept secret. There is no doubt that the real problem Cullingford and Senior (and their successor for a time) had to face was not architectural but the unwillingness of the governors to take them into their confidence and admit them to their committees before decisions were made.

Mr. Senior's aims were similar to Cullingford's: 'to train the mind, not to fill it - to set before us a vision of greatness - to teach devotion to truth, however unpalatable'. He withdrew from the scene at Easter 1959. After a term's interregnum during which R.H.S. Hatton acted as headmaster, Robert Glover took office in the following September. This was the second time there had been three headmasters in a year. Mr. Glover had taught at Ampleforth, was head of classics at the King's College, Canterbury, and since 1953 had been headmaster of another Haberdasher property, Adams' Grammar School, Newport, Shropshire.

He arrived in 1959 to take over a new classroom block, a proposed assembly hall, and a school whose numbers had reached their highest ever with 464 boys. On the debit side he succeeded to a school which was no longer represented on the Headmasters' Conference, a serious situation which was not to be resolved until his election to that body after the resignation of the chairman of the governors, two traumatic years later.

At speech day in 1969 Robert Glover put before parents and the public two cautionary suggestions for them to consider. The first concerned the tendency of governments to treat Education as a political shuttlecock. 'It is assumed that every citizen, because he has had first-hand experience of being in school, is an expert in education. This is perhaps rather like saying that anyone who has ever had appendix removed is an expert in heart-transplant surgery'. That being the case, parents should look carefully at all political concepts where education is concerned, and if in doubt, return to first principles and the fundamental object of education, 'to find out what a boy is good at, and to help him to become better at it'.

His second suggestions was that parents should be cautiously sceptical of the advice churned out by the vast army of 'educationalists', supposed experts who have never actually taught anyone and who wrap their theories in portentous and incomprehensible language, in which state it is rarely effective. But it then becomes simplified into catch-phrases which become dangerous when taken over by progressives. Parents should make sure that they know where that progress is leading them. Is it to the boy becoming better at what he is good at, so gaining 'the assurance and self-confidence that will enable him to meet what life brings ?' If it is not, they should bring their 'astringent common-sense to bear', and reject it.[23]

He then began a prolonged battle against the proposal by the government to phase out the direct grant system. The conversion of the secondary modern to a comprehensive would *ipso facto* do away with reserved places at Monmouth School. There were 124 boys with tuition fees paid by the county councils in 1972. Although this facility was not under immediate threat, he reminded parents in 1974 that 'if direct grant goes, the school which has served the boys of Monmouth area for nearly four centuries, will suddenly become for many families financially prohibitive'.[24]

In the following year Mr. Glover returned to the offer by the government that if direct grant schools accepted voluntary status, the school would continue to receive county funds. But this was only if the school undertook 'to admit pupils without reference to ability or aptitude'. The LEA proposal was for a single sixth form accepting pupils from both the Haberdasher schools and a new comprehensive. 'This would make the most effective use of highly qualified teachers, would provide pupils with more subject options, and would give the best chance of achieving economically viable classes'.[25]

This left the school with three choices: total independence, absorption in the state comprehensive system, or closure. It was quickly assumed that Monmouth would remain independent, and that the governors would review the whole system of scholarships. The Old Monmothian Club then came to the rescue and set up a committee, supported by Lord Brecon and Sir Derek Ezra, which raised £100 000 for a scholarship fund in ten weeks. At Robert Glover's last speech day he was able to tell parents that, 'If independence is going to bring any sort of crunch it will be in five or six years' time when the talented and versatile Mr. Bomford will be available to deal with it'.[26]

Mr. Glover achieved a great deal. He opened three new boarding houses, at Weirhead, Tudor and Chapel House, and founded a flourishing preparatory school at The Grange. The sports centre, language laboratory and art and handicraft workshops added to the amenities. On the cultural and social level, the Merlin Music Society flourished, Mrs. Glover became a leading light in local drama, founded the Luncheon Club and started visits by the boys to the Cheshire Home. The centenary of the rugby club was celebrated, and at long last sixth form dances with the girls' school became regular occasions. He had done much to make it what a candidate for the headmastership called 'one of the friendliest schools in the country'.[27]

He was followed in 1977 by Nicholas Bomford who came from Wellington. He was an historian, had been captain of shooting at Oxford, and referred to the Glover era as a daunting one for anyone to follow. It was certainly a decade when clubs and societies of every description flourished. Chess had been played for a hundred years, ever since R. Petrie, an Old Monmothian, drew with the world champion before being drowned in his twenties.[28] Bird watching, contemporary music, stamp collecting, photography, model railways, orienteering, astronomy, conservation, canoeing, sailing and sub-aqua activities flourished. So did the Union Society, Athenaeum, and Christian Fellowship. Each had its followers and a section in the pages of *The Monmothian*.

Building continued apace, including plans for a new science block on the site of the old Town House. It was to be three stories high and would enhance rather than detract from the view from the A40 approaches or from across the Wye. The architect, Mr. Ling, had worked at Rugby and Stowe and hoped to produce something 'exciting and constructive'. He enthused about the string courses preventing the building from looking monolithic and devised the curious corner windows because 'over-fenestration wasted energy'.[29] A time capsule made of lead from Town House roof was buried beneath it and the building was opened by Princess Margaret in 1983. A year later a design and technology centre was authorised to complement it.[30]

The value of these new facilities was emphasised when the school won the national competition for Young Scientist Masterminds (and £1000) at the Natural History Museum in 1992. The school had been warned as early as 1967 by Admiral of the Fleet, Sir Jasper John, to beware of computers. 'Do not make their existence an excuse to give up thought and the exercise of judgement'.[31] Unlike much speech day advice, it seems to have sunk in, as it was not until 1981 that Mr. Bomford bashfully announced that the school had bought two, and he was wondering how to ensure that the boys were made familiar with this 'micro-electronic revolution'.[32] He need not have worried; computers soon began to arrive by dozens.

A major reorganisation within the school took place in 1981 with the abolition of form masters for all ages except the first form. Thereafter each boy was allocated an academic supervisor who would remain with him for the rest of his time in school. The Assisted Places Scheme still caused concern and Mr. Bomford had told the Welsh Office that he was willing to conform provided it remained complimentary to the maintained sector. They had examined over two hundred boys in 1981 and admitted twenty. But he warned parents of the continuing threat to independent schools and the importance of a combined defence through membership of the Independent Schools Information Service.

But his time at the school was short and in 1982 he moved to Uppingham and later to Harrow. He was followed by Rupert Lane, a native of Ross-on-Wye, who came from Marlborough where he had been housemaster and coach to the 1st XI. His predecessor had encouraged co-operation with other schools in drama and music. *Oliver*, *Patience*, and *Guys and Dolls* had been produced with the help of girls from Monmouth Comprehensive and John Kyrle High School, Ross. Rupert Lane continued the tradition with a performance of *The Winter's Tale* with players from Monmouth School for Girls, at the Malvern Festival Theatre.[33] Societies continued to proliferate: a Coin Society, a Graves (Robert) Society and a 14-25 Musical Society for pupils and ex-pupils in that age group from all schools as an alternative to the Merlin. Archery, basketball and a trampoline club added variety to the traditional games.

Challenge of Industry Conferences started in 1978 for the two Haberdasher schools, which were joined by the Monmouth Comprehensive sixth form in the 1980s. The conferences are now shared between the three schools and have proved a valuable social innovation. An adventure centre was opened in 1987 at Aberangell in Snowdonia. Tours abroad became common; rugby to New York, South Africa and Canada; cricket to Sri Lanka; rowing to Ghent and art to Florence. Parties travelled to the Karakoram, to Malka Hilda in Somalia for the Monmouth Aid Project which in ten years had raised £65 000, to Scotland for the Mountain

Marathon, and to Osaka in Japan. In 1991 over one hundred boys were engaged in European exchanges and over seventy on the Duke of Edinburgh's Award Scheme.

The Old Monmothian Club celebrated its centenary in 1986 having commissioned two large murals for the school chapel. They represent the Crucifixion and the Resurrection and were designed by Adam Kossowski, a wartime companion of Otto Maciag, the head of art. The design was converted to clay by Otto Maciag and Michael Tovey and dedicated by the Bishop of Monmouth on 3 October 1987.[34]

Threats by Labour and the Liberals against the Assisted Places Scheme continued to cause concern, and as usual advice and orders continued to rain down on the schools from the bureaucrats and politicians above. In 1988 the National Curriculum landed to a hurricane of protests from those expected to carry it into the classroom. But Rupert Lane thought it would be 'political folly to distance ourselves from it', so the governors asked Adrian Barlow, Director of Studies at the school, to produce a report for the governing body on the current trends in education (1985 - 1995).[35] This was especially necessary for Monmouth, a small town in which the schools, public, comprehensive, primary, private and infant, probably provided more employment than any other occupation.

He described many of the problems, past, present and future; the raising of the school leaving age from 14 to 16; the end of direct grant and the 11 plus; assessment of performance; and renewed emphasis on vocational training. In this last field Monmouth Comprehensive had a head start, and although Monmouth School had decisively rejected the LEA's offer of a combined sixth form for the three Monmouth secondary schools in 1974, the closer organisation of the two Haberdasher sixth forms was now necessary to counter the growing threat from the state sector.

The problem of co-ordinating these sixth forms was made more difficult by the different ways the teaching was organised; Monmouth School for Girls had a five day week and nine periods a day; Monmouth School had a five and a half day week and seven periods a day. Adrian Barlow suggested that the governors set up a policy committee to review the philosophies of the two schools and to decide when practical collaboration over a joint sixth form might begin. Before this could be implemented, there would have to be agreement between the schools, the staffs and the parents that the benefits of such change would outweigh traditional prejudice in favour of single sex schools.

A prolonged period of discussion between the two schools ensued, bolstered by committee reports, statistics provided by a firm of professional consultants, and the varied opinions of the teachers and parents. The outcome was a letter from the chairman of the governors to every parent stating that all sixth form pupils would have access to all subjects taught, even if in only one school, teaching resources would be shared, syllabuses jointly planned, and timetables revised. Flexible boarding would be introduced, non-academic activities combined and the boys would continue with a five and a half day week and the girls with a five day one. Although this was not very different from the proposals of the LEA in 1974, the two schools set about making these innovations possible.

But innovations are not everything, and Rupert Lane, in the midst of so much time devoted to implementing government proposals, asked, as so many previous headmasters had done, what Education was really about. Not GCSEs and A levels, he thought, but attempting to refine the five senses; the sense of pride in what was undertaken, a sense of urgency to get things done, a sense of right and wrong, a sense of wonder at the great things in life, a sense of fun, and for a sixth sense, sensibility towards others.

Mr. Lane was appointed headmaster of Ridley College in Canada in 1994. His successor is Timothy Haynes, surmaster of St. Paul's School, London.

If one asks what aspects of school life have done most to refine these senses, and at the same time bring together a school and a town which were often at odds, a high mark must be given to music and the theatre. Fine productions of *Murder in the Cathedral* in local churches and frequent appearances of the school choir have set high standards. Several headmasters have been good musicians and encouraged music-making. The old board school in Glendower Street has been converted into a music centre which was opened by Jane Glover, the artistic director of the London Mozart Players and the daughter of a previous headmaster. Under Jonathan Holmes the Haberdashers' Music Festival has become a regular feature; combined school orchestras flourish; and the Merlin Music Society continues to fill the school hall.

In 1992 the school provided five boys to sing in the Welsh National Opera production of *The Magic Flute* in Cardiff, and in 1993 the school choir took part in a performance of Mahler's Third Symphony with the BBC National Orchestra of Wales. In the same year a party of fifty-two choristers travelled to sing at Newark, Lincoln Cathedral and York Minster. The concert band represented Wales at the European Wind Band Festival in 1990 and won a gold medal three years later in Manchester. Three chamber ensembles reached the finals of the

Monmouth Schools Orchestra, 1992

The school choir with Jonathan Holmes, 1994

National Chamber Competition in London in 1993. The only school with more representatives was a special music centre drawing from schools over a wide area. There have been many instances nearer at hand when school musicians have delighted local audiences, a good example being the performance of Purcell's chamber opera *Dido and Aeneas* in the garden of Treago Castle in 1993. Sir Thomas Armstrong, Principal of the Royal Academy of Music, said at the opening of the Assembly Hall in 1962, 'Music and Art are the durable expressions of man's hopes and aspirations ... music is the common ground of communication'.

Music, buildings, academic excellence, sporting triumphs, the dedication of the staff, the sympathy and encouragement of the company and the governors: all are of importance to a school such as this, as are the services of those, like Dennis Morgan, who have given a lifetime to make the school function comfortably and efficiently - porters, typists, matrons, boatmen, cleaners, groundsmen and gardeners. But if one asks what has been the real key to its status throughout the three hundred and eighty years of its existence, it must be the thirty headmasters and their wives. The buck stops with them, as does the glory. Doctor Busby, who was headmaster of Westminster School from 1640 almost until his death in 1696, was renowned for his flogging ability. He taught Dryden and Locke, and claimed to have birched sixteen future bishops at a time when they numbered more brilliant men than ever before or since. He always wore his Monmouth cap, even when showing Charles II round his school, 'for it would not do for my boys to suppose that there existed a greater man than Doctor Busby'. He was equally firm with his Westminster parents when he told them:

> 'The Fathers among you govern the Nation
> The Mothers govern the Fathers.
> The Boys govern the Mothers,
> And I govern the Boys'.[36]

References

[1] SLB. 9/11/1932.
[2] MB. 20/7/1928.
[3] SLB. 9/11/1932.
[4] MB. 12/7/1929.
[5] MB. 3/7/1931.
[6] MB. 1/7/1932.
[7] MB. 13/2/1931.
[8] MB. 27/2/1931. 3/4/1931.
[9] MB. 3/8/1934.

[10] MB. 18/12/1936.

[11] MB. 28/7/1939. and LB. 6/12/1936.

[12] Draft of pamphlet, *Monmouth 1939-1944*, probably by C.H. Dobinson in VA.

[13] MB. 12/7/1940.

[14] MB. 8/7/1942.

[15] MB. 7/7/1950.

[16] Speech Day 1955.

[17] Speech Day 1954.

[18] Speech Days 1973, 1974, 1975.

[19] Published 1992.

[20] Shrine of Remembrance, W.R. Irving, 1948.

[21] *Monmothian,* 1990. Article by P.J. Mathew and R. Parry.

[22] *The Story of the Merlin Music Society. The First 21 Years, 1963-1984.* Ed. S.A. Bucknall.

[23] Speech Day 1969.

[24] *Monmothian*, 1972, 1974.

[25] T. Morgan, *Monmouthshire Education, 1889-1974*, p.126.

[26] Speech Day 1977.

[27] Ibid.

[28] J.N. Becket, 1897-1901.

[29] *Monmothian* 1977.

[30] *Monmothian* 1984.

[31] *Monmothian* Sept. 1967.

[32] *Monmothian* 1891.

[33] *Monmothian* 1983.

[34] See *The Murals in Monmouth School Chapel* by Reverend N.F.M. Morris, 1987.

[35] Published Nov. 1990.

[36] Quoted by Rupert Lane, Speech Day 1984.

Monmouth School 1995

KEY

RECEPTION

Headmaster's Office	R1
Porter's Lodge	R2
Bursary	9
Chapel	24
Common Room	13
Dining Hall	8
Glover Music School	11
Lecture Theatre	16
Library	25
Red Lion Block	7
School Hall	10
School Shop	9
Sports Centre	5
The Grange	27

BOARDING HOUSES

Chapel House (off map)	28
New House	1
St. James House	29
School House	20
Weirhead House	2

DAY HOUSES

Dean House	7
Gwent House	21
Hereford House	22
Monmouth House	23
Town House	12
Wye House	7

DEPARTMENTS

Art	17
Design & Technology	19
English	15
Geography	6
History	7
Information Technology	14
Modern Languages	6
MountJoy Maths Centre	26
Sciences	18

SPORTS FACILITIES

Boathouse	30
Gymnasium	4
Pavillon	32
Sports Ground	33
Squash Courts	3
Swimming Pool	4
Tennis Courts	34
Wyebridge Cottages	31

Appendix A: Headmasters

1615	John Owen
1617	Humfrey Crewys
1639	Nathaniel Taynton
1657	Robert Brabourne
1658	Robert Frampton
1663	John Harmer
1663	Charles Hoole
1664	William Morrice
1672	Thomas Bassett
1687	Thomas Wright
1691	Thomas Bassett (restored)
1713	Andrew Cuthbert
1723	James Birt
1738	Baynham Barnes
1758	John Crowe
1780	Thomas Prosser
1793	John Powell
1823	William Jones
1828	John Oakley Hill
1832	George Monnington
1844	John Dundas Watherston
1859	Charles Manley Roberts
1891	Edward Hugh Culley
1906	Lionel James
1928	Christopher Fairfax Scott
1937	Wilfred Roy Lewin
1941	Noel Chamberlain Elstob
1946	Cecil Howard Dunstan Cullingford
1956	John Robert Murray Senior
1959	R.H.S. Hatton
1959	Robert Finlay Glover
1977	Nicholas R. Bomford
1982	Rupert Lane
1995	Peter Anthony
1995	Timothy Haynes

Examination Papers.

MIDSUMMER, 1870.

Divinity.

1. When did the Flood take place? What were the terms and what was the sign of the covenant made with Noah? Quote and explain his prophecy respecting his sons.

2. With respect to (1) Abraham and Lot, (2) Jacob and Laban, state how they were related, under what circumstances they separated, and under what circumstances they again met.

3. Adduce passages from the Book of Genesis which record prophecies or types of the Messiah.

4. From whom did the following nations spring, and where were their possessions?—the Philistines, the Midianites, the Edomites.

5. Give an account of the institution of the Passover, and the observances with which it was celebrated. Establish from Holy Scripture its typical import. What were the other great feasts of the Jews?

6. How were the Israelites guided through the wilderness? By what sign were they commanded to advance? Mention some particular occasions on which their wants were miraculously supplied.

7. Into what great national sin did the Israelites fall immediately after the delivery of the law from Mount Sinai? Relate the conduct of Moses on this occasion.

8. Give an account of the miracle on the day of Pentecost. What significance is there (1) in the time of the occurrence; (2) in the miraculous appearance itself?

9. In what passages in the Acts is Philip the Evangelist mentioned?

10. What advice was given by the several speakers at the Apostolic council? What decision was arrived at? Account for the prohibitions imposed on the Gentile Christians.

11. Narrate the occurrence which took place during St. Paul's first visit to Philippi and Thessalonica.

12. Trace the course of St. Paul's voyage and journey to Rome, and give the dates of his arrival and death.

ARITHMETIC.—I.

1. Write down in words 5,104030,012017.

2. How many tons, cwts., etc., are there in as many ounces as there are seconds in a week ?

3. Find by *practice* the cost of 113 tons, 17 cwt., 1 qu., 11 lb., at £2 3s. 9½d. per cwt.

4. A certain article is taxed 6d. per lb. If the taxation be reduced 10 per cent. the consumption of the article will be increased by one-seventh. The expense of collecting the tax is three-farthings per lb. The income arising from the tax is £12,200. Find what it will be after the above changes.

5. Is it cheaper to buy wine here at £1 10s. a gallon, or to import it, paying 18s. for the wine per gallon, for carriage ⅛ of the price of the wine, for warehousing ⅓ of the cost of the carriage, with a Customs duty of 25 per cent. on the original cost of the wine, and losing ⅟₁₂ of the wine by leakage ?

6. What is the rule for reducing a vulgar fraction to a decimal. Reduce $\frac{355}{113}$ to a decimal. State and prove the rule for reducing a recurring decimal to a vulgar fraction. Reduce .02134 to a vulgar fraction.

7. Find the compound interest of £5503.4375 for 4 years at 5 per cent.

8. Find the alteration of income occasioned by shifting £3200 from the 3 per Cents. at 86¾ to 4 per Cents. at 114⅞, the brokerage being ⅛ per cent.

9. Explain discount and find the discount on £1000 due 2 years hence at compound interest.

10. The price of diamonds *per carat* varies as their weight. If a diamond of 3 carats is worth £75 what is the value of one of 2 carats ?

11. In a constituency in which each elector may vote for 2 candidates, half the constituency give 1 vote for A, but give their second vote to B, C, D, E, in the proportions of 4, 3, 2, 1 (*i. e.* four times as many vote for B as for E, and so on) ; of the other half of the constituency two-thirds give their first vote to B, but give their second vote to C, D, E, in the proportions of 3, 1, 1 ; half of the remainder vote for D and E, and 540 do not vote at all. Find the order on the poll and the whole number of electors.

(Monmouth Grammar School, June, 1872.)

ARITHMETIC.—II.

1. Write down in words 4608930762. Also write down in figures five billions, eight hundred and seven thousand five hundred and three millions, six hundred and fifteen thousand, and three.

2. Write down all the numbers of four digits you can form with the digits 3, 4, 0, 6, and add them together.

3. If a bale of cotton weighs 11 cwt. 1 qr. 17 lb. and cotton costs $7\frac{1}{4}d$. per lb., find what the cost of 561 bales will come to, including a charge for packing of £1 10s. per bale, and another of £5 per ton for carriage.

4. Define a vulgar fraction and prove that if the numerator and denominator be multiplied by the same quantity the value of the fraction will not be changed.

5. Simplify the following—

    (1.) $\frac{16}{17}$ of $5\frac{4}{7}$ of $\frac{901}{109}$ of $13\frac{1}{8}$.

    (2.) $\frac{4}{13}$ of £5 6s. 8d. $+ \frac{9}{7}$ of £39 $- \frac{3}{10}$ of £1 5s. 1d.

    (3.) 15.411 of £441 15s. $-$ 6.9869 of £14 6s. 3d.

6. A man's income is £930. He pays one-eleventh of his income as rent, an income-tax of $7d$. in the pound, a poor-rate of 1s. 3d. in the pound on his house rent ; what will his net income be ?

7. What decimal of a sovereign is $\frac{3}{10}$ths of 13s. ?

8. Multiply .0701 by 700.01 and divide 8886.66 by .0037.

9. A cannon ball moves with a velocity of 1000 metres per second. The metre contains 39.37079 inches. Find what decimal of a mile its velocity per second is, and also express a second as a decimal part of an hour.

(Monmouth Grammar School, June, 1872.)

143

INORGANIC CHEMISTRY.

N.B.—Any *eight* questions in this paper may be answered, but *not more than eight.*

  I. Explain and illustrate the difference between a *mechanical mixture* and a *chemical combination.*

 II. Give the simplest form of the mercurial barometer. On what does the height of the mercurial column depend?

III. How is the composition of water determined by synthesis and decomposition?

 IV. State briefly the theory by which Dalton explained the laws of chemical combination.

  V. Under what different forms does carbon exist?

 VI. Show how chlorine is prepared, and state its principal properties.

VII. How is nitric acid prepared? Give the process in words and symbols.

VIII. Give the ordinary method of preparation of gaseous ammonia, and state its most important properties.

 IX. Explain briefly the construction and principle of the Davy lamp.

  X. Give your reasons for considering the air to be a *mechanical mixture.*

 XI. Give the symbol and atomic weight of each of the following elements :—Oxygen, Carbon, Chlorine, Nitrogen, Sulphur.

XII. Give the names of the following formulæ :—
N_2O, NH_3, CO_2, CH_4, HCl, CO, C_2H_4, CN, $HClO_4$.

(*Monmouth Grammar School, June,* 1872.)

NATURAL PHILOSOPHY.

1. Enumerate the chief properties of matter, and illustrate the following, viz.—*compressibility, elasticity,* and *inertia.*

2. Distinguish between general and special properties of matter. Define *density,* and state to which class it belongs.

3. Define the terms *velocity, equilibrium, momentum.* Explain clearly, with illustrations, what is meant by saying, that " action and reaction are equal and contrary."

4. State the law of acceleration, and show how it can be proved by experiment. What is the real meaning of *weight ?*

5. Give instances of molecular force. How does this force differ from *gravity ?*

6. Describe the different varieties of the lever, and show how to estimate its mechanical effect. What is the effect of the invention called the *governor ?*

7. State and account for the hydrostatic paradox. Give an account of the screw propeller, showing how it acts. What is *specific gravity ?*

8. Show how to construct a barometer, describe its different varieties, and demonstrate the effect which the atmosphere has upon it.

9. Explain the terms *pitch, intensity, timbre,* as applied to sounds. On what does the rate of velocity of sound depend ? And what law governs the rate of vibration of a string ?

10. Give the laws of reflection and refraction, and show, in connexion with the structure of the eye, how spectacles cure the defects of sight. Describe the Gregorian telescope.

(*Monmouth Grammar School, June,* 1872.)

ENGLISH LANGUAGE AND LITERATURE.

1. Show the defects under which the English orthography labours. Give examples where (*a*) the same sound is expressed by different letters ; (*b*) different sounds are expressed by the same letters. Give some directions as to dividing words into syllables.

2. What do you mean by the word *gender*, as applied to a noun or pronoun ? Give the feminines of *boar, colt, Czar, marquis, executor*, and the masculines of *heifer, hind, witch, madam, belle*.

3. Distinguish between Qualitative, Quantitative, and Definitive adjectives, giving examples of each. Explain exactly what is meant by the comparison of adjectives. Is it correct to speak of the prefixing of words like *very, exceedingly, rather, somewhat*, &c., to the adjective, as a mode of comparison ?

4. What is the derivation of the word mood ? Define its meaning, and state what moods exist in English. Do you number among them a *potential mood* ? If not, why ?

5. Analyze the sentences in the following passage :—

" Among the tribunes of the year was P. Sulpicius, a master of lofty and pathetic eloquence, who had been a friend of the unfortunate Drusus, and was animated by bitter enmity against Q. Pompeius Rufus, Sullas's colleague in the consulship. This was the person whom old Marius now selected as his political agent, as he had formerly chosen Saturninus. Marius held up before his ardent imagination the treasures of Mithridates, promising that if the command were transferred to himself he would employ the wealth of the Pontic King to relieve the Roman debtors."

6. Criticise the following sentences, and point out mistakes where any exist :—

(*a*) It is good sort of people who are tempted to it.

(*b*) This impatience and repining is natural to the young.

(c) There was not a philosopher's door but opened to him of
     its own accord.

(d) We can easier descend than ascend.

(e) Whom do you suppose called on me to-day ?

(f) He ordered no one to leave the room.

7. Describe the plot of the *Merchant of Venice*, and state the
sources from which the different parts were derived by Shakespeare.

8. Give a criticism of the character of Shylock, illustrating it
by appropriate quotations from his speeches in the play.

9. In what senses are the following words used in Shakespeare ?
—*Conceit, commodity, nice, danger, posy, remorse, quaint, manage,
counterfeit, jump with, fond.*

10. Comment on any peculiarities in the construction of the
following passages, and quote parallels where you can :—

(a) "I urge this childhood proof."

(b) "Her name is Portia, nothing undervalued to Cato's
     daughter."

(c) "O father Abram, what these Christians are,
     Whose own hard dealings teaches them suspect
     The thoughts of other !"

(d) "Are there balance here to weigh the flesh ? "

(e) "We have been praying for our husbands' healths,
     Which speed, we hope, the better for our words."

11. Explain by derivation the words *surgeon, argosy, prize,
predicament, mere, " I wis," fill-horse, fancy.*

12. Describe the plan of Paradise Lost, and give an analysis of
the Second Book.

(*Monmouth Grammar School, June,* 1872.)

MIDSUMMER, 1870.

French.

I.

1. Give the different forms of the comparative degree of inferiority.

2. Give the place of the personal pronouns when direct and indirect objects to a verb ; 1. when the verb is in a compound tense ; 2. when the verb is in the imperative affirmative.

3. What are the rules applying to *le, la, les,* as personal pronouns ?

4. What are the rules applying to *quelque ?*

5. How do you construe a sentence—1. When *personne* stands as subject ? 2. When *personne* stands as object to a verb ?

6. What difference is there between possessive adjectives and possessive pronouns ? Give them.

7. Give the demonstrative adjectives and demonstrative pronouns.

8. How are ordinal adjectives generally formed ? Give examples and exceptions.

9. Give the present and past participles; the indicative present, past definite, and future; the imperfect and pluperfect subjunctive of the verbs *avoir, être, déroger, venir, décevoir, pendre,* in the first person singular.

10. How do you conjugate a passive verb? Give the past definite indicative and past conditional of the verb *être battu*.

11. How do you conjugate a reflective verb? Give the absolute future and imperfect subjunctive of *se défendre*.

12. How is a verb conjugated when used—1. Interrogatively? 2. Negatively? 3. Interrogatively and negatively?

    N.B.—Give examples, illustrating each rule.

II. Correct the faults in the following sentences :—

Jalousie produit haine (*h. a.*), envie, et les autres passions qui causent le malheur de homme (*h. m.*).

Mon père est un médecin, mon frère un avocat, et moi je serai un soldat.

Les fleurs ne sont pas joli, mais elles sentent bonnes.

Les troîsième et quatrième étage de cette maison ont été réparés.

Est-ce je, ou bien est-ce tu ?

Cette maison est louée tres chére, bien que ce soit neuf et grand.

Chacun vreudront à leur tour réciter leur leçon.

Beaucoup désire savoir, mais fort peu veut apprendre.

Nous avons arrivé un quart d'heure trop tôt.

Quant à je, qu'importe à moi !

Mon oncle a amené de Londres deux chevaux qui fera l'admiration de la toute ville.

Appendix C

Extracts from tabular digest of returns furnished by trustees and headmasters of endowed grammar schools in reply to the printed inquiries of the commissioners, 1864/67.

	Abergavenny	Monmouth	Usk
Population	4621	5783	1545
Boarders	2 (?)	0	5
Day boys	14 (?)	100	19
Masters	2	4	2
Parents' occupations: *A	17%	10%	-
B	83%	80%	-
C	0	10%	-

*A Independent, professional, mercantile
B Farmers, shopkeepers
C Artisans, labourers

Knowledge on admittance	Reading	Reading Writing	Reading Writing
Numbers taking:			
History	4	86	23
Geography	20	100	23
English grammar	20	76	23
English literature	0	14	0
English composition	7	11	15
Reading	23	100	7
Writing	23	97	21
Drawing	0	2	0
Religious instruction	23	100	All
Latin	13	24	0
Greek	2	8	0
French	4	0	0
Arithmetic	23	97	23
Mathematics	2	26	0

	Abergavenny	Monmouth	Usk
Best subjects in opinion of headmaster	English French Latin	Commercial for present class of boys	Those prescribed
Best subjects in opinion of parents	Arithmetic, French, geography, and book-keeping	Commercial	-
Corporal punishment	In School	In presence of school	Publicly
Power of monitors	None	Report Evils	Report Offences
Size of playground	40 ft.square	Half an acre	Third of an acre
Head's difficulties	No house, small stipend of second master	Bad English used by boys out of school.	-

Appendix D: Admissions by area, 1828-68

	Monmouth	Monmouthshire	Gloucestershire	Herefordshire	Outside
1828	54	8			
1829	16	1			
1830	4	2			
1831	24	3			
1832	19	5			
1833	33	10			
1834	20	5			
1835	18	6			
1836	33	4			
1837	15	3			
1838	19	5			
1839	15	8		1	
1840	41	7	8	2	
1841	13	9			
1842	23	3	1	3	
1843	39	3	8	4	
1844	24	11	19	1	1
1845	23	5	1	4	1
1846	17	4	2	2	
1847	17	2		2	
1848	27	5		2	
1849	17	7			
1850	24	1	2		
1851	12	4	2		
1852	19	3	1	1	
1853	21	7	9	6	
1854	15	7	4	1	
1855	17	11		2	
1856	16	5	1		
1857	21	5	4	1	
1858	24	3	3	3	
1859	22	6	2	1	
1860	20	2	1	3	
1861	25	4	1		
1862	11	9	4	1	
1863	11	9	5	2	
1864	18	8	5	2	
1865	12	5	2	1	
1866	16	12	2	2	
1867	7	5	3	1	
1868	6	4	2	1	

(MCA. D 262.19)

Bibliography

Allsobrook, D.	*Aspects of the History of Monmouthshire Grammar Schools in the Nineteenth Century.* (Gwent Local History, No.55. 1983). *Schools for the Shires: The Reform of Middle-Class Education in Mid-Victorian England.* (Manchester, 1986).
Anon.	*A Short History of Monmouth School.* Undated.
Archer, Ian W.	*The History of the Haberdashers' Company.* (Phillimore, 1991).
Carlisle, N.	*A Concise Description of Endowed Grammar Schools in England and Wales.* (1818).
Corten, A.	*Aspects of the History of the Grammar Schools in Monmouthshire During the Nineteenth Century.* (Gwent Local History, No.53.1982).
Eveleigh, M.	*Hitting the Right Note.* (1992).
Heath, Charles	*Accounts of the Ancient and Present State of the Town of Monmouth.* (Monmouth, 1804).
Hill, C.	*The English Bible and the Seventeenth Century Revolution.* (Allen Lane, 1993).
Jordan, W.K	*The Charities of London, 1480-1660.* (1960).
Kissack, K.E.	*Monmouth, The Making of a County Town.*(Phillimore, 1975). *Victorian Monmouth.* (Ledbury, 1980). *Haberdashers' Monmouth School for Girls, A Centenary History.* (Gomer Press, 1992).
Littlewood, A.S.	*Three Hundred Years of Monmouth Grammar School.* Ms. in SA (234/RO 92480).
Morgan, T.	*Monmouthshire Education, 1889-1974.* (Cwmbran, 1988).
Morris, N.F.M.	*The Murals in Monmouth School Chapel.* (Monmouth, 1987).
Pitt, K.M.	*Monmouth School in the 1860s.* ND.
Seabourne, M.	*Schools in Wales, 1500-1900.* (Gee & Son, 1992).
Seaver, P.	*The Puritan Lectureships: The Politics of Religious Dissent, 1560-1662.* (Stanford, 1970).
Tompson, R.	*Classics or Charity. The Dilemma of the 18th Century Grammar School.* (Manchester, 1971).
Toulouse, H.C.	*Monmouth School Rugby Football Club. 1873-1973.* (Newport, 1973).
Ward, H.A.	*Monmouth School. 1614-1964. An Outline History.* (London 1964).
Warlow, W.M.	*A History of the Charities of William Jones at Monmouth and Newland.* (Bristol, 1899).
Webster, J.R.	*The Welsh Intermediate Education Act of 1889.* (The Welsh History Review, Vol.4 No.3, 1969).

The Monmouthshire Merlin, The Monmouthshire Beacon, The Monmouthshire Gazette, The Monmothian, The Dasher.

IN MEMORIAM 1914-1919

OLD MONMOTHIANS KILLED IN WORLD WAR I

1914
Horace Watkins

1915
Walter Breakwell
Thomas Clements
Arthur Davies
Ellerton Davies
David Dudley
Bertram Evans
Samuel Evans
Francis Farran
Frederick Harris
Horace Herd
Vernon Matthews
Charles Payne
Charles Rooke
Vivian Watkins
George Weatherhead
William Webb

1916
Euan Arnott
Ernest Bricknell
Henry Davies
John Davies
Sydney Hockaday
Rhys Hughes
Ivor Jones

Arthur Latham
Clive Page
Louis Phillips
William Rea
Harold Redler
Henry Rees
Horace Richards
Edgar Teague
Horace Thomas

1917
Ferdinand Adamson
Sidney Ayers
Frank Bailey
Colin Baumgarte
William Bennett
Walter Bianchini
John Bolton
Ralph Bond
Alfred Bowen
Thomas Broughton
Denis Busher
Sidney Davis
Horace Dowdeswell
John Evans
Charles Freeman
Peter Heyworth
Alexander Lowe

Roy Rawlins
Eric Saunders
Eric Thomas
Victor Ursell
John Williams

1918
Thomas Aston
John Bastock
Reginald Bolton
Charles Chapman
Frank Edwards
Alexander Foott
Percival Guest
Leonard Horne
George Howell
Geoffrey Osborne
Arthur Phipps
John Sayes
Mervyn Watkins

1919
Glynne Bateson
R.G.L. Cumbley
Ernest Cunliffe
Frank Greenland
J.M.D. Mills
Reginald Parry
Henry Reilly

IN MEMORIAM 1939-1946

OLD MONMOTHIANS KILLED IN WORLD WAR II

1939
Reginald Tucker

1940
Adrian Bouwens
Geoffrey Hartland
Millham Lloyd
Stanley Morgan
Richard Wilson

1941
Arnold Akers
Peter Brawn
Raymond Clark
Percival Harris
Phillip Harvey
Thomas Little
John Neate

1942
Peter Armstead
Howard Baker
Kenneth Daniel
Terrence Humphries
Clifford Kidd

Roy Leng
Harry Morgan
Gilbert Reynolds
David Toms
Alfred Watkins
Allen Wood
Gerald Young

1943
James Aston
Eric Benison
Douglas Bown
George Crum
Camm Davies
Wyndham Davies
Harold Durrant
Ewart Jones
Leslie Jones
William Mountjoy
Norman Roach
Raymond Spierling
Clifford Walters
Dennis Welsh

1944
Kenneth Beecher

Alfred Blake
Richard Cleaver
Edward Coldicutt
Raymond Lang
Glynne Lewis
Paul Maynard
Douglas Meek
Haydn Phillips
Maurice Powell
John Richards
Howel Richards
Norman Silk
Peter Walters
David Whitcombe
Gordon Williams
Paul Williams

1945
Noel Burrows
John Hutchings
Ronald Jones
Stephen Palmer

1946
Donald Riley

Index